Second Edition

Australian Football

STEPS TO SUCCESS

Andrew McLeod
Adelaide Football Club
Australian Football League

Trevor D. Jaques, MA
Adelaide Football Club
Australian Football League

Human Kinetics

Library of Congress Cataloging-in-Publication Data

McLeod, Andrew, 1976-
  Australian football : steps to success / Andrew McLeod, Trevor D. Jaques.-- 2nd ed.
    p. cm.
  Jaques is sole author of previous ed.
  ISBN 0-7360-6005-7 (soft cover)
  1. Australian football. I. Jaques, Trevor D., 1943- II. Title.
  GV947.M37 2006
  796.336--dc22   2005018238

ISBN: 0-7360-6005-7

Copyright © 2006, 1994 by Human Kinetics, Inc.

The Web addresses cited in this text were current as of October 12, 2005, unless otherwise noted.

Acquisitions Editor: Jana Hunter
Developmental Editor: Cynthia McEntire
Assistant Editor: Scott Hawkins
Copyeditor: Patsy Fortney
Proofreader: Bethany J. Bentley
Graphic Designer: Nancy Rasmus
Graphic Artist: Kim McFarland
Cover Designer: Keith Blomberg
Photographer (cover): © The Advertiser
Art Manager: Kareema McLendon
Diagram Illustrator: Roberto Sabas
Figure Illustrator: Patrick Griffin
Printer: Sheridan Books

Human Kinetics books are available at special discounts for bulk purchase. Special editions or book excerpts can also be created to specification. For details, contact the Special Sales Manager at Human Kinetics.

Printed in the United States of America   10 9 8 7 6 5 4 3 2 1

Human Kinetics
Web site: www.HumanKinetics.com

United States: Human Kinetics
P.O. Box 5076
Champaign, IL 61825-5076
800-747-4457
e-mail: humank@hkusa.com

Canada: Human Kinetics
475 Devonshire Road Unit 100
Windsor, ON N8Y 2L5
800-465-7301 (in Canada only)
e-mail: orders@hkcanada.com

Europe: Human Kinetics
107 Bradford Road
Stanningley
Leeds LS28 6AT, United Kingdom
+44 (0) 113 255 5665
e-mail: hk@hkeurope.com

Australia: Human Kinetics
57A Price Avenue
Lower Mitcham, South Australia 5062
08 8277 1555
e-mail: liaw@hkaustralia.com

New Zealand: Human Kinetics
Division of Sports Distributors NZ Ltd.
P.O. Box 300 226 Albany
North Shore City
Auckland
0064 9 448 1207
e-mail: info@humankinetics.co.nz

Australian Football

STEPS TO SUCCESS

◪ Contents

◪ Climbing the Steps to Australian Football Success

In Australia the word *football* has always referred to a number of different sports. If you came from the eastern side of the country, *football* meant *rugby*, although even that wasn't clear-cut. If you were of middle or upper class and went to private school, it was *rugby union*. To those of the middle to working class with a public school background, it was likely to be the more rough-and-tumble, less genteel *rugby league*. For those of recent European origin, *football* was *soccer*. American expatriates knew *gridiron* as football, and the Irish had their *Gaelic football*.

The southern states are the traditional home of the game unique to Australia—Australian football. When South and Western Australians, Victorians and Tasmanians talk of football, or *rules* (it used to be called Australian Rules Football), it is this form they refer to. If they do mention the others (and most don't), they refer to them as *rugby, soccer* and *gridiron*. Devotees of those other codes generally call Australian football *AFL football* or simply *AFL*.

Notwithstanding its relatively small population and proliferation of football codes, internationally Australia has had considerable success in both versions of rugby, and Australian soccer players can be found in many English, Scottish and European club soccer teams. Hence internationally, it is understandable that football in Australia is generally assumed to be either rugby or soccer. However, the preeminent form of football is the uniquely Australian variety. Different as it is, Australian football engenders all that is exciting, good (and bad), appealing and attractive to people who play and watch any other code of football. It has now been played long enough to establish traditions, rivalries and legends, the things that ignite passions and fuel fanaticism. In short, it is a great game. More players play it and certainly more watch it (both live and on television) than play and watch the other codes. Australian football has lost its southern bias and is now played at the elite level throughout Australia.

Although the popularity of Australian football has spread, surprisingly, resources are still fairly limited, both for players and for teachers and coaches. This book is designed to help fill some of that void. This second edition has been written to be at a level beyond that of the first edition. Although it addresses the player directly, it is meant to be of value to the coach as well. It contains more drills for larger groups that coaches may incorporate in their formal training sessions while still providing the individual player the help to develop his own skills by himself or with a small group of mates.

Considerable debate continues as to the best order in which to learn the skills of Australian football. As in most sports, practice and the mastery of one skill may often depend on the abilities of others. For example, unless a teammate can put the ball in the correct position to mark, a player will have difficulty practising marking.

The steps presented in this book are not set in rigid order (although having possession of the ball is obviously a prerequisite for disposal), but their order is based on some logic. They are not necessarily designed to be separate and discrete. For example, step 3, Gathering the Ball, while highlighting the essentials in learning the various techniques of this aspect of the game, incorporates other techniques in the drills (in this case, handballing and kicking) to give players a chance to practise picking up the ball. This overlap is deliberate. Learning a technique in isolation is not efficient, and techniques are not used in isolation in game situations. Only in context does a particular technique truly become a skill.

Each of the steps includes practice drills. Some drills are intended for a player practising alone, some require two players who are practising together, some drills are for small groups of players to practise together either at formal training or in free time, and some are for larger and more experienced groups and are to be included as drills related to game situations. These will generally be organised and controlled by the coach and done at formal training sessions. At times the drill may need to be modified to suit the players. Conversely the size of the area being used may need to be reduced to suit the abilities of the players.

Drills also graduate from simple to complex; players are able to progress from one to the next as technique improves. Of course, the number of ways to rehearse various skills is limited only by the imagination, and the drills given for one activity can often be used for or adapted to another.

Drills need to be done at maximum intensity. A player accustomed to moving comfortably to the ball will almost invariably be beaten to it in a game by a player who trains at a greater intensity. To this end, then, you will find our text liberally sprinkled with terms such as *attack the ball, take possession, aggressive running, direct approach, confidence, intensity* and *commitment*. Often players can make the drills competitive or

more pressured by seeing how many they can do in a set time or competing against a partner either in speed or scoring. Several examples are given, but players should get into the habit of inventing scoring and competitive systems to place themselves under just that little more pressure. What was the score last time? What is the record? What is the score to beat? Questions like these are also useful in setting goals, giving feedback and providing motivation. Practising kicking is valuable, but practising kicking at a specific target (such as a post) is more so.

In today's game, players need to be 'two sided'. From the earliest stages of learning, players should learn and practise the skills of the game on both sides of the body. A player who can kick with only one foot, handball or spoil with only one hand, leap off only one foot, lead to only one side, turn in only one direction and so on is not only less efficient and less effective but also easier to defend against. Therefore, players should vary drills to practise in different directions and from different sides.

Don't be afraid of making mistakes. Careful players play without flair, and only seldom do they make something out of nothing or do the impossible like the truly great players. Place yourself under pressure and don't be frightened of making mistakes. Learn from them and correct them, and in doing so improve your game.

This book is aimed at one major goal—developing a committed, complete player, one who gains maximum benefit from practice by pushing himself to extend his skills and who is prepared to do more than exist in the comfort zone of repeating what he can do at a speed and under the pressure that does not place him or the technique at risk.

After an introductory section that includes an explanation of the game of Australian football, the book is divided into steps that focus on the basic skills you need in order to play Australian football. As you progress through the steps, the seemingly isolated skills become linked so that when you get to the steps on the game plan and positional play, you will be better able to play your part as an effective and confident team member.

While going through the steps, you should follow the same procedure for each step:

1. Read the explanations of what the step covers, why the step is important and how to execute the step's focus, which may be basic techniques, concepts, tactics or all three.

2. Follow the numbered illustrations showing how to position your body to perform each basic technique successfully. Where appropriate, these illustrations are presented in three phases: preparation (starting position), execution (performing the technique) and recovery or follow-through (finishing position).

3. Look over the missteps that may occur and the corrections.

4. Read the directions for each drill. Practise accordingly and record your scores. At the end of the step, you will be asked to review your scores to determine whether you are ready to move on to the next step.

5. Have a teacher, coach, parent or skilled player watch you perform each technique and evaluate your skill. Ask this person to suggest improvements.

Some drills at the end of each step will only be able to be done at formal practice with other members of the team. These will not have goals or ratings but will enable you to practise in game-like situations under the eye of your coach who will provide feedback.

Finally, there is a step on training effectively. This step is directed at both the player and the coach or teacher to maximise the time available at formal training sessions. As players become older and more experienced, the steps throughout the book, although still appropriate and practical, are more likely to be done at organised training sessions.

We have been fortunate to have been involved in the game at the highest level and experienced the thrill and excitement of ultimate success at that level. That same thrill, excitement and sheer enjoyment are also seen in players of all ages and in all competitions. Because of that and the enthusiasm and encouragement of our teachers and junior coaches, we began our journey that culminated at the MCG on the traditional last Saturday in September, the AFL Grand Final.

If by preparing this book we are able to help and encourage others to take up and play the game, improve their game and seek to become one of the elite, it has been worthwhile. But more so, if this book in some small way helps young people achieve some success, enjoyment and fun through playing Australian football, then we have gone some way to repaying the game that has meant and given so much to us. It is a great game, the greatest game of all. We hope this book will play its part in ensuring that it continues to be so.

◼ Acknowledgments

Whereas the errors, mistakes and omissions in this book are ours alone, the ideas, concepts and practices are not. They are a combination and development of our experiences during years of involvement in football. We wish to pay tribute to those family members, teachers and coaches of ours over the years who in their own ways have made their contributions to this book. Their thoughts and ideas are embodied in this book. Their enthusiasm and support have influenced our thinking and desire to share them with others.

◧ The Sport of Australian Football

Australian football is but one of the codes of football played in Australia. It is different in many ways from the others, not the least being its uniqueness to Australia. If you have ever tried to explain the game to someone unfamiliar with it, you know how difficult it can be. Descriptions often start with comparisons, such as, it is faster than soccer, it is more exciting than rugby union, it is as tough as rugby league, and, it requires more endurance and versatility than American football. But such comparisons are unfair to the game and to the codes with which it is being compared.

Similarly, inclusive descriptions fall well short of conveying what the game is like. Australian football is much more than a mixture of the vigour of rugby, the skill of soccer, the strength and speed of American football, the high leaping and ball control of basketball and the speed of Gaelic football, even when considering its unique contribution of long and accurate kicking and spectacular high marking. Some would argue that Australian football embodies much of what we think about Australia itself: rugged individualism and energetic and sometimes brash and daring head-on aggressiveness. The game is played on fields resembling the country itself—big, open and uncluttered. It evolved when the country was young and populated predominantly by men thrown together during a time of excited immigration to a new country with few cultural, artistic or sporting opportunities.

HISTORY

Australian football has roots common with other kicking sports. When discussing the game's origin, we could begin with the ancient Chinese, Indian, Australian aboriginal and Gaelic kicking games. Or we might start with the development of soccer, or that famous day at Rugby School when William Ellis picked up the ball and ran with it.

It has been convenient to note the similarity with the Irish game and to suggest that Australian football is a direct descendent of Gaelic football. The argument is even more compelling because the game developed at the same time that a large number of Irish were making the dash to the Victorian goldfields.

However, even though the game does have its closest modern link with Gaelic football, there now appear to be more arguments against this direct connection than for it. Many now assert that its origins are more likely to be found in Aboriginal games. Or perhaps it is just as we now know it—a truly unique Australian invention.

Ultimately the platform was there for Henry 'Coldy' Harrison and Thomas Wills to formulate the Australian style of football. Believe it or not, the game was established to be more 'genteel' with less risk to life and limb than the 'tougher' sport of rugby. However, in typical Australian fashion, the game was played with so much enthusiasm and gusto that it quickly developed into the fast, vigorous, hard-tackling, rough-and-tumble game we now know.

Australian football probably predates other modern forms of football. The game was devised initially as a form of fitness training for Victorian cricketers to enable them to beat those from New South Wales. Reported games of 'football' had been played from the 1820s, but what form it took at that time is questionable.

The 7th of August 1858 is credited as the day the first official match of Australian football was played between clubs or schools. It was in Melbourne between St. Kilda and Melbourne Grammar schools. It grew from there, but the traditional rivalry between the two major colonies has had an enduring effect on the game. Victoria has remained the strength of Australian football. Until quite recently, New South Wales, along with Queensland, resisted the intrusion of Australian football in a major way, and the game played (and still plays) a secondary role to the rugby codes. This is despite the fact that the team from Queensland won three championships in a row beginning in 2001.

The game spread west and south where strong followings were established in South Australia, West Australia and Tasmania. These states, along with Victoria, still are the major proponents of the game, but as of 2005 it is played all over Australia by over 510,000 registered players. There are competitions in each of the states, the Northern Territory and the Australian Capital Territory. With the formation of the Australian Football League (AFL) with teams from each of the mainland states and with regular games programmed for Tasmania and the territories, with carnivals for teams for all the states and territories at the senior, junior, amateur and school levels and for a fledgling women's competition, the game can now be accurately described as national.

Although played as a demonstration sport at the Melbourne Olympic Games in 1956 and with exposure through the Sydney Olympics in 2000, Australian football is isolated internationally and is likely to remain so even though the game is seen on foreign television and Australian teams have played recently in England, Canada, the United States, South Africa and New Zealand as part of an extension of regular competition. There are annual games at senior and junior levels between Australian and Irish teams playing a hybrid game of Australian and Gaelic football. Fledgling Australian football leagues also exist in the USA, Ireland, Canada, Denmark, Nauru, Papua New Guinea, Samoa, Japan and New Zealand. The International Cup provides a triennial competition among these leagues. Australian football's relative isolation does not, however, detract from the game, which with its free-flowing style, high scoring and exciting body contact will pack stadia and fairly lay claim to being one of the, if not the, most exciting games of all.

THE GAME

The game's uniqueness is seen in many ways. It is played between two teams of 22 players each, 18 of whom can be on the field at once. Players are freely interchangeable at any time. Unlike most other field games, there is no offside rule. Except after a minor score (which is unique in itself, rewarding a near miss) and when the ball is kicked out of the field of play on the full, possession of the ball is continually contested.

The field itself (figure 1) is atypical in shape and size, being determined by the amount of space available. (The original ground at the present MCG is reported to have been over 550 metres long.) Its large size is one of the reasons

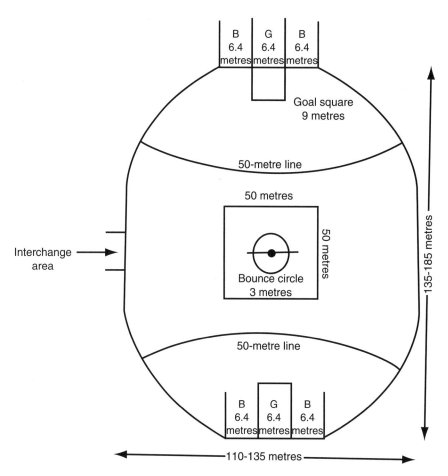

Figure 1 A typical football field.

it is not played internationally, where few playing arenas can accommodate it. Historians suggest that some early games were played on rectangular fields, but the game is now one of the very few field games not played on a rectangular field or court.

The primary object of the game is to score more points than the opposition. Points are scored by moving the ball over lines between four uprights, each 6.4 metres apart, at either end of the field. If the attacking team kicks the ball between the middle two uprights without the ball touching any other player or the posts, a *goal* (worth 6 points) is awarded.

A single point is scored for a *behind*, when the ball passes between the outer posts on either side of the goal or when the ball has been touched by any other player prior to passing through the middle uprights. This rewarding of players for a near miss on goals is a feature unique to Australian football. This rule was developed to prevent the attacking side from gaining too great an advantage when the ball was being thrown in after going out of bounds. Hence, 1 point was awarded to the scoring team, and possession of the ball was given to the defending side.

Other features pertaining to scoring that are peculiar to Australian football are that there is no maximum or minimum height of the goals and that a defender cannot score a goal for the opposition (an own goal). In senior games it is not unusual for each team to score in excess of 100 points.

The ball is moved around the field quickly through kicking, handballing (throwing the ball is not permitted) and running (with its own brand of dribbling during which the ball must be bounced or touched on the ground every 15 metres). Kicks are often long, covering 50 or 60 metres, with pinpoint accuracy. Catching a kicked ball allows the player to take a free kick if he so chooses without the risk of being tackled.

This aspect of the game adds much appeal as players leap, often in groups, trying to catch the ball on the full, not uncommonly using other players as step ladders to get high into the air.

Each game consists of four quarters, the length of which is determined by the governing body, typically depending on the age and level of the players. At senior levels, the quarters are of 20 minutes' playing time with time added on whenever there is a stop in play. There are no timeouts during the quarters, but coaches communicate with players and make substitutions at any time by using a runner to convey messages. If the scores are tied at the end of the game, the game is drawn.

FIELD POSITIONS

One change to the game in recent years has been the tactical positioning of players on the field. Offensive players take up a variety of positions, and defensive players position themselves accordingly. At the senior level of Australian football, players freely change positions during the course of the game, partly in an attempt to confuse the opposition and partly to avoid (or force) unwanted player match-ups.

No matter where players are placed, however, players in today's game need to have both offensive and defensive skills. There are specialist positions, but a feature of a good player is the ability to play many positions. Modern parlance describes some players as *midfielders* or *on-ballers*, illustrating the more nomadic positional play of some team members. Because of the distances covered by some of these players, plus coaches trying to establish a strategic advantage, several players might be assigned these roving duties, which can extend over the whole ground. These roving players exchange positions and roles with other similar players (called rotations) to give them a rest or confuse the opposition.

Nonetheless, teams are still traditionally placed, and it is valuable for those beginning the game to know the positions on the field. Figure 2 shows how a team is usually named to line up. The players have opponents in the opposite positions marking them. For example, the centre half forward will be marked by the opposing team's centre half back.

The game is started and restarted after each goal by a central umpire who bounces the ball in the small circle in the centre of the field. At this time only four players from each team—usually, but not required by the rules of the game, the centre player, the ruckman, the ruck rover and the rover—may be in the centre square. This is the closest to any offside rule there is in the game.

EQUIPMENT AND ATTIRE

The most important piece of equipment for the game is the football. The ball is made of leather, usually reddish-brown for day play and yellow for night matches. The official rules state that the ball should be as close as possible to the standard shape with the size being 570 by 740 millimetres and weighing between 450 and 500 grams. Children play with a smaller and lighter ball to help them develop correct kicking and handling skills.

The uniform consists of a jumper (with or without sleeves), long socks, shorts and football shoes. Each player has a number on his jumper. Although the players must have different numbers, the numbers do not correspond to their positions as in some football codes.

Shoes are normally of two styles. One style has screw-in replaceable sprigs that give greater grip when the ground is softer and the grass is long. The other popular style has rubber soles with moulded sprigs or cleats, which are generally worn on firm turf and when the ground is hard.

Use of protective equipment is minimal, although some players wear shin guards inside their socks. Although not widespread, a recent

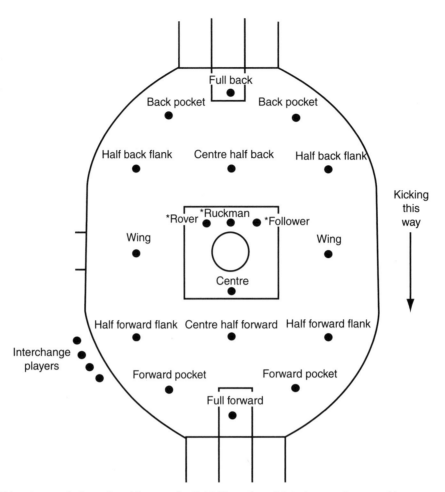

Figure 2 Traditional map of players' positions on the field. The roles of the players whose positions are preceded by an asterisk (*) are to roam the whole ground (they are sometimes called 'followers' or 'on-ballers' because they follow the ball around the ground); they have no set positions as such but may be given specific tasks by their coach. They might change with players from set positions during the game when those players need a rest. The interchanged players on the sidelines are now no longer backup players in the case of injury. They are integral team members often forming part of the on-ball rotations.

innovation, particularly at the junior level, has been the introduction of rubberized head protectors. The most commonly used guard is the mouth guard; its use should be widely encouraged to protect teeth and gums and reduce the likelihood and severity of some concussions.

GAME RULES

The rules of Australian football are not overly complex, nor are there a great number of them. As skills, tactics and drills are described throughout the book, the appropriate rules will be discussed. What follows is a brief explanation of the main playing rules. To test your knowledge of the rules, take the quiz on page xix.

At the senior level, the game is played over four quarters of 20 minutes each, with time being added on for delay of game, player injury, recovery of the ball as a result of scoring and out of bounds. This time on will be signalled by the central umpires but recorded and added to normal time by the timekeepers.

The game is started at each quarter and restarted after each goal by one of the central umpires bouncing or throwing the ball up in the centre circle. The ruckmen must be within the larger circle at the time the ball is bounced or thrown up. At this time only four players from each team are permitted in the centre square and no player may be in the centre circle until the ball is bounced. Infringements to these rules result in a free kick to the opposition from the centre circle.

A goal (6 points) is scored when the ball is kicked over the goal line by a player of the attacking team without the ball touching a player or goal post. To score, the ball must completely cross the goal line.

A behind (1 point) is scored when the ball passes over the goal line in any way other than just described, touches or passes over a goal post or passes over a behind line without touching or passing over a behind post. A defending player cannot score a goal for the opposition. If he kicks or takes the ball over either the goal or behind line, a behind is scored for the attacking team.

After a behind has been scored, any player from the defending team kicks the ball back into play from within the kickoff lines in front of goal. The player kicking the football into play may, provided he has kicked the football clear from his hands, regain possession and play on from the goal square. This is rarely seen, however; most kickoffs are kicked long out of the scoring area with all other players being at least 5 metres from the kickoff line when the ball is kicked.

To go out of bounds, the ball must completely cross the boundary line. If the ball goes out of bounds other than on the full from a kick or directly from a kickoff without being touched by any player, a boundary umpire throws the ball back over his head towards the centre of the ground into play. If the ball goes out of bounds on the full from a kick, directly from kickoff without being touched by any player whether on the full or not or from being deliberately knocked or carried over the boundary line, a free kick is awarded to the nearest player from the opposite team.

Gaining Possession

In the official rules, the Spirit of the Laws statement relating to possession says, 'The player who makes the ball his sole objective shall be given every opportunity to gain possession of the ball' (15.1). This statement is intended to help players and umpires in the interpretation and application of the rules of football.

A mark is allowed when the ball is caught on the full from a kick that has travelled at least 15 metres and is not touched in flight. The player taking the mark may go back behind the mark and take his kick or may play on immediately. In going for a mark, a player may be awarded a free kick if he is

Modifications for Young Players

To encourage young players to participate in games and to develop their skills without the fear of being hurt, many junior football associations use modified rules. These modifications may include the following:

- The number of interchange players is unlimited.
- The ball can be bounced only once before disposal.
- Players cannot soccer the ball off the ground.
- A ball kicked out of bounds is awarded to the opposing team (if it is touched before going out, a ball up is contested).
- After scrimmages the game is restarted by a ball up contested by any two players of similar build near the scrimmage.
- For the youngest groups, tackling the player with the ball is not permitted.
- To encourage greater participation, the number of players per team is restricted.
- The players who can score are limited, and all scoring must be from within a certain zone.

- blocked or shepherded when the ball is more than 5 metres away;
- pushed, bumped or shepherded when he is in the air attempting a mark;
- pushed from behind except when the opponent is legitimately attempting to mark, spoil or play the ball;
- held, tripped or charged by an opponent; or
- hit on the head, neck or top of the shoulders by an opponent trying to contest the mark.

In general play, in contesting for possession of the ball, a player will be awarded a free kick when he is

- held in any way when not in possession of the ball;
- shepherded when the ball is not within 5 metres;
- pushed from behind in any way;
- tripped, charged, struck or kicked;
- pushed, bumped or shepherded in the face, head, neck or on the shoulders;
- in possession of the ball and tackled below the knees or on or above the shoulders including the collar of the football uniform; or
- held once he has legally disposed of the ball.

Playing in Possession

Once a player possesses the ball, the rules pertain to that possession. Again, the statement relating to the Spirit of the Laws helps in the understanding, interpretation and application of these rules: 'The player who has possession of the ball and is held by an opponent shall be given a reasonable time to kick or handball the ball' (15.1).

A player is deemed to be in possession of the ball if he is holding the ball, bouncing it while running or lying on or over the ball. He may possess the ball for an unlimited time provided he is not held by an opponent. If he is running with the ball, he must bounce it or touch it on the ground once every 15 metres. Once tackled,

however, the player in possession must attempt to dispose of the ball *immediately* by kicking or handballing. He will be deemed to have had prior opportunity to legally dispose of the ball and will be penalised as he is tackled.

A player in possession of the ball will have a free kick awarded against him for

- not disposing of the ball within a reasonable time when held by an opponent;
- dropping the ball or bouncing it when tackled;
- holding the ball if he has the ball pinned or held to him by a tackle and has had a reasonable chance to dispose of the ball prior to being tackled;
- throwing or handing off the ball (the ball must be held in one hand and hit with the clenched fist of the other hand);
- kicking the ball over the boundary line on the full without it being touched by another player (here the free kick is awarded where the ball crosses over the boundary line rather than where the kick was taken);
- deliberately forcing the ball over the boundary line; or
- running more than 15 metres with the ball without touching or bouncing it on the ground.

In most cases, free kicks are taken at the spot where the infringement took place. An exception is when a player is infringed against after he has disposed of the ball. Here a foul after disposal will result in a free kick from where the ball landed. (If the kick has scored a behind, the infringed player is given the choice of accepting the score or having another kick.)

Under the Spirit of the Laws, the central umpires can allow play to continue after an infraction (even though a free kick should have been awarded) when stopping play would penalise the team offended. This is indicated by the umpire calling 'play on, advantage!' and applies only to free kicks, not to marks.

In the same spirit, to keep the ball and game moving and to prevent wasting time and the deliberate professional foul, a central umpire may award a 50-metre penalty following a mark or free kick if in his opinion

- a player is infringed against after a mark or free kick has been awarded;
- the player on the mark refuses to stand on the mark or encroaches over the mark;
- the player deliberately wastes time by knocking the ball away from the player who has been awarded a free kick or who has marked the ball or by not returning the ball on the full to the player who is to take the kick; or
- the player on the mark holds the player who is to take the kick.

Taking the Free Kick or Kick From a Mark

When a player takes his kick, only one opponent is allowed to stand the mark. No player is allowed in the protected area as the kick is taken (figure 3).

When kicking, the umpire will direct the player to kick over his mark. However, if and when the player moves off the direct line over the mark to the goal, the umpire will call 'play on' and defensive players may attempt a tackle.

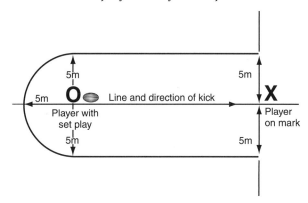

Figure 3 Player X stands the mark. Player O has the free kick or mark.

Officiating

The rules of any game are meant to create order. Umpires interpret and apply rules during a game. Umpires, players, coaches and indeed spectators need to know the rules and understand their spirit as well as some of the difficulties in their application. All serious players should have a

copy of the official rules of the game. These are available from the various state football leagues and associations or directly from the AFL.

Many of the rules in Australian football are open to interpretation; for example, rules pertaining to scoring and whether the ball is in or out of play depend on the judgment of the umpires. As Bill Deller, former National Director of Umpiring, once said, 'Umpiring Australian football is the most difficult adjudicating task in the world. The game is played on the biggest of all sporting arenas; it has the largest number of players; it is the fastest moving and allows more physical contact . . . over a longer time period than any other football code. Added to this, the laws are interpretive and the umpire is continually called upon to make judgments. . . . The fact that the laws are so interpretive is a unique feature of the game'. Things haven't changed since Deller made that statement.

Most sports have some rules that require interpretation and judgment, usually quickly during the game. Australian football is no exception, and it is here that disagreement and conjecture arise. It is important in making good judgments to keep in mind the spirit of the rules, which have been designed to protect the player who is prepared to go and get the ball and in so doing makes the ball his sole object. Once a player has the ball, the rules give him a reasonable time and reasonable protection to dispose of it legally.

Conversely, the defender must not be disadvantaged by any rule or its interpretation to the extent that he becomes hesitant to apply a tackle. Defenders who use skill and determination to meet their opponents and tackle within the rules are rewarded by the rules of the game. So, both attacking and defensive skills are encouraged by the spirit of the rules. Indeed, several rules penalise players who waste time, who deliberately force the ball out of play and who do not contribute to the swift movement of the ball up and down the length of the world's largest football field.

At the senior level, the game is controlled by seven umpires. Three central umpires interpret and administer the playing rules, and two boundary umpires adjudicate when the ball goes out of play and, if necessary, throw it back into the field of play. Two goal umpires have the responsibility of deciding whether a goal or behind is scored, signalling as such and then recording and keeping the score.

Rules Quiz

What is the umpire's decision? Score 1 point for each correct answer. (Answers are on page xix.)

1. Player A tackles player B, firmly pinning his arms to his sides. Player B drops the ball.
2. Player A has taken a mark and player B comes in and knocks the ball out of his hands.
3. Player A hands (gives) the ball to his teammate while being tackled by player B.
4. Player A holds the ball for longer than five seconds but is not tackled.
5. Player A runs 10 metres, handballs over player B's head, retakes the ball without it hitting the ground and runs another 10 metres before kicking.
6. The full back kicks out after a behind and the ball goes over the boundary line without anyone touching it.
7. Player A leaps from behind player B and pushes with his hands on player B's shoulders to get more height and take a spectacular mark.
8. Player A has the ball and is about to be tackled by player B. Just before the tackle, player A bounces the ball and does not have it in his hands when tackled by player B.
9. Player A is running towards the boundary line chased by player B. He slips and while falling knocks the ball over the boundary line so that player B cannot get it.
10. Player A is tackled around the neck and the ball drops to the ground. His teammate, player B, picks up the ball and kicks it down the ground in the direction of another teammate.
11. The ball is halfway across the boundary line but is knocked back by a player before it completely crosses the line.
12. Player A, while desperately defending, turns and kicks. The ball comes off the side of his foot and goes through his opponent's goals.
13. Player A marks the ball and goes back to take his kick. As he runs in to take his kick, he slips, falls and drops the ball, which an opponent picks up.
14. Player A marks the ball and goes back to take his kick. He sees a teammate and makes to give a handball but changes his mind and does not release the ball.
15. The ball is kicked at goal and goes directly over the goal post. What does the goal umpire signal?

Your score ___

AUSTRALIAN FOOTBALL TODAY

Australian football is governed by the AFL, which also organises and conducts the major club competition comprising 16 teams. But it does far more than that. It also has assumed the responsibility for nurturing and developing the game.

Australian Football League
GPO Box 1449N
Melbourne, Victoria 3001
Australia
www.afl.com.au

To nurture and develop the game, the AFL supports nearly 200 full- and part-time development officers who manage the junior football 'Auskick' and oversee coach and umpire accreditation, school clinics and talent identification and development programmes throughout Australia. It also conducts 'AFL Kickstart' within indigenous communities in Northern Australia, which is designed to promote health and lifestyle issues through involvement in football. It organises national age championships as well an annual international tour for under 17s against an Irish team playing 'International Rules', a combination of Australian and Gaelic football. There is also a joint AFL/Australian Institute of Sport football academy. The AFL also provides support for state league competitions. Each of the states and territories has its own league for the administration of the games in their area. Amateur leagues, associations and school organisations ensure that competitions are available for all levels, ages and abilities that wish to compete.

Each year players and representatives of the 16 AFL clubs visit regional locations that are holding community camps. In 2005 more than 100,000 people experienced the camps at primary school or secondary school visits, super clinics, hospital and aged care visits, community forums and functions.

Beyond football, throughout the year clubs and players spend many hours supporting community issues that may range from the Beyond Blue project focusing on youth depression to the Walk Against Diabetes.

Answer Key

Rules Quiz

1. Holding the ball. Free kick to player A.
2. Award player A the mark and charge player B a 50-metre penalty.
3. Free kick to player B. The ball cannot be handed to a teammate. It must be handpassed by punching the ball.
4. Play on.
5. Running too far without the ball touching the ground. Free kick to player B.
6. Free kick to the opposition from where the ball crossed the boundary.
7. No mark. Free kick to player B for interference above the shoulder.
8. Holding the ball against player A, who is deemed to be in possession. Free kick to player B.
9. If it was accidental, throw-in. If the umpire interprets that it was deliberately hit over the boundary line, free kick to player B.
10. Free kick to player A for over the shoulder but play on for team's advantage.
11. Play on because the ball did not completely cross the boundary line.
12. One point scored for the opponents.
13. If the umpire has not called 'play on' and player A is still behind his mark, he retakes his kick.
14. The umpire will call 'play on' and player A can be tackled.
15. One point (a behind) as the ball must clearly go between the goal posts or their extensions.

◧ Key to Diagrams

A, B, C, etc. = Players

———————▶ = Player running

◠ = Ball

– – – – – –▶ = Ball kicked

·············▶ = Ball handballed

ℓℓℓℓℓℓℓℓℓ▶ = Ball rolled

—+++++++++▶ = Ball thrown

·············▶ = Ball hit or knocked

▲ = Marker

T = Target

⌓ = Goal

O = Defensive team

K = Kickoff team

W = Wingman

RK = Ruckman

F = Follower

CHF = Centre half forward

HFF = Half forward flank

FP = Forward pocket

FF = Full forward

R = Rover

C = Centre

Ball Handling

Whatever the sport, proficient players practise, and continue to practise, the basic skills of the game, particularly if the game involves a ball. Professional golfers hit hundreds, even thousands, of practice shots just to keep their swings in the groove. A basketball player handles the ball whenever possible, lobbing it from hand to hand, bouncing and dribbling, shooting at a goal from many angles and distances. The cricketer likewise handles the ball continually. The legendary Don Bradman spent countless hours hitting a ball as it bounced irregularly off a tank stand.

Although practice alone doesn't make perfect (practice makes permanent; perfect practice makes perfect), confidence in handling the equipment does enhance and hone a player's technique, making it easier to develop it into a skill. Because of the odd shape of the ball in Australian football, it is probably even more important than in other sports to handle the ball as much as possible early on, both during instructional times and outside the formal setting. Many AFL footballers, the best in the country, are given a ball by their clubs to have on hand, and it is not unusual to see a player just handling the ball at home, at work, watching TV and at other spare times. Watch the accomplished players as they stand and bounce the ball, kick it and then catch it, handball it into the air and catch it, spin the ball, toss it from hand to hand and the like.

AUTOMATIC BALL HANDLING

During a game, players don't have time to go through the checklist of things they must do to pick up the ball, to handball it or to catch or kick it. Similarly, as they gather or mark the ball, they need to do it cleanly and then move it into the correct position for disposal.

As the ball comes, the better player can adjust automatically—hands and body move to the correct position, fingers spread, and eyes don't leave the ball. Such automatic responses leave time and concentration for the other aspects of the game—pressure from an opponent, getting the ball to a moving teammate, adjustment for the conditions, tactical considerations and the like. Skill and confidence in ball handling, brought about by many hours of practice, are the first step in giving players the time and confidence to attend to other things that go towards making a champion.

Mistakes in ball handling are self-evident. The ball is not taken in the hands cleanly and may be dropped altogether. Ball handling must also be accurate and includes the concise and efficient disposal of the ball once it has been taken. Most of the missteps in ball handling will be dealt with in the following steps on gathering and disposing of the ball. However, some general ball-handling errors and their causes will be addressed here.

Misstep

The ball hits your hands and bounces free.

Correction

Take the ball with soft hands. If your hands are stiff, the ball is more likely to bounce off them.

Fundamental to any ball-handling skill is to watch the ball. Focus on it even to the extent of looking for the lacing on the top of it. As you do so, move into position as soon as possible as the ball comes towards you. Taking the ball while both the ball and you are moving, while essential in games, makes clean ball handling more difficult and therefore more of a risk. It is very important that you position your hands early, watch the ball into them so as not to snatch at it and take it with soft hands. Stiff fingers and palms increase the likelihood of the ball bouncing from them.

Misstep

You have trouble catching the ball with a particular catch.

Correction

Are you watching the ball? Do you need to deliver the ball more accurately? Remember, ball control happens in both the delivery and the catch.

The drills that follow have been designed to help develop ball-handling skills. You can try these drills straight away. Perform them whenever you can. However, don't ever think that you have mastered handling the ball. You can always try to perform the drills faster, for a longer time, in a different position, in a different direction or with something added to make the drill slightly more difficult to help improve your ball handling.

With each drill, practise it first, several times if need be, and then test yourself. Although we have given these drills very simple scoring systems, you can continually test yourself by devising competitions or your own scoring schemes. Come back to this step over and over again to retest yourself, but also try to make the tasks more difficult for yourself and, knowing your abilities, make up new ones.

A coach will need to adapt these drills to the level of his players by varying distances, numbers and speed. He should also make sure that the players use an appropriate size ball. For younger and smaller players, a smaller ball (and sometimes a softer one) will help.

Ball-Handling Drill 1. *Toss and Catch*

Toss the ball into the air and catch it. This can be varied in a number of ways, such as the height of the throw or the spin of the ball—end over end away (topspin), end over end towards (underspin), spiral spin, helicopter spin.

The catch can be similarly varied—one hand, two hands, catch above the head, catch on the chest or catch as low as possible (perhaps as the ball hits the ground). What about catching the ball after doing a complete turn, while sitting or with one or both feet off the ground? Can you catch it behind your back? Trap the ball on the ground with one or two hands as it hits the ground.

Success Check

- How comfortable do you feel handling the ball?
- What do you hear as you take the ball? If you hear a slapping sound, it means your fingers and hands are not relaxed and the ball could bounce out.
- Watch the ball for as long as you can and preferably right into your hands.

Score Your Success

Toss and catch the ball 10 times. Give yourself 1 point for each successfully completed toss and catch. Vary the type of toss and the type of catch as you become more confident.

Your score ___

Ball-Handling Drill 2. *Hand to Hand*

Toss the ball from hand to hand, varying the speed, height and hardness of the throw and the distance between your hands. Try the basketball hook shot, looping the ball high over your head from your right side to catch with your left hand on your left side. Repeat, throwing the ball from your left side and catching it with your right hand on your right side. Have five throws and catches from both sides.

Success Check

- Lob the ball accurately from hand to hand.
- Watch the ball all the time.
- Be confident in your ability to catch the ball with both left and right hands.

Score Your Success

Toss and catch the ball 10 times, 5 times from each hand. Give yourself 1 point for each successfully completed toss and catch. Vary the type of toss and the type of catch as you become more confident.

Your score ___

Ball-Handling Drill 3. *Figure Eights*

Stand with your feet a little more than shoulder-width apart. Put the ball on the ground and roll the ball around your body first one way and then the other (figure 1.1a). Roll it in a figure-eight pattern around and between your feet (figure 1.1b). Now pass the ball around your legs and then in a figure-eight pattern, keeping the ball at knee height (figure 1.1c).

Practise by yourself at first and then with a partner. Have races to see who can be the first to do 10 of each of the activities.

Figure 1.1 Figure eights: *(a)* Roll the ball on the ground around your body; *(b)* roll the ball on the ground in a figure-eight pattern around and between your feet; *(c)* pass the ball in a figure-eight pattern between your legs at knee height.

Success Check

- These are competitive drills, so you are trying to beat your partner.
- Have the ball under control at all times.
- Develop a rhythm to make the ball movement smooth and controlled.
- Increase the pace of the ball as you become more confident and establish the rhythm.

Score Your Success

Roll the ball around your body on the ground 10 times, changing direction after 5 times. If you beat your partner, score 5 points. Roll the ball around and between your feet in a figure-eight pattern 10 times. If you beat your partner, score 5 points. Pass the ball between your knees 10 times. If you beat your partner, score 5 points.

If you are by yourself, try to set records in each of these by seeing how many laps you can get the ball to do in a set time and then try to beat your own score.

Your score ___

Ball-Handling Drill 4. *Bent-Knee Pass*

Pass the ball around your body at waist height (figure 1.2a). Alternately, pass the ball under and over your legs while walking in place with high knee lifts (figure 1.2b). Now try the same exercise while sitting, keeping your heels off the ground and your knees bent (figure 1.2c). Pass the ball rapidly around both legs. Don't forget to practise going in both directions.

Figure 1.2 Bent-knee pass: *(a)* Pass the ball around your body at waist height; *(b)* pass the ball over and under your legs while walking in place with high knee lifts; *(c)* pass the ball around both legs while sitting.

Compete against a partner to see who is the first to get 20 circuits of the ball, changing direction after 10.

Success Check

- Keep the ball under control at all times.
- Grip the ball as you pass it from hand to hand. Don't throw it.

Score Your Success

If you complete 20 circuits around your waist before your partner does, you score 5 points. If you complete 20 circuits over and under your knees before your partner does, you score 5 points. If you complete 20 circuits around your knees while sitting before your partner does, you score 5 points.

If you are by yourself, you might try to set records in each of these by seeing how many laps you can get the ball to do in a set time and then try to beat your own score.

Your score ___

Ball-Handling Drill 5.   *Clenched Fist Punch*

Hold the ball with one hand and use the clenched fist of your other hand to punch the ball into the air to catch it. Vary the height and switch hands. Try variations such as always catching the ball in the hand it was hit from. Are you able to spin it so that you always catch it with the seam pointing directly away from your body? Try allowing only one spin before you catch it. You can test this by always being able to see the lacing on the top of the ball when you catch it.

To Increase Difficulty

- Add a little difficulty by setting yourself targets such as one and a half, two or more spins before catching the ball. To accomplish this, you might have to catch the ball closer to the ground or do higher, loopy handballs that spin more slowly.

Success Check

- Are you equally confident and proficient with your left and right hands?
- Progress from the simple to the more difficult drills.

- Do five successive catches without error before moving on to the next most difficult drill.

Score Your Success

Handball and catch the ball 10 times, 5 each with your left and right hands. Give yourself 1 point for each successfully completed handball and catch. Try this another 10 times but vary the type of handball and the type of catch as you become more confident but still alternating left and right hands. Give yourself 1 point for each successfully completed handball and catch.

Your score ____

Ball-Handling Drill 6. *Bouncing*

Regularly practise bouncing the ball. This is not a skill used often in games, but it is an essential lead-up to kicking and is invaluable to ball handling. Bounce the ball on the forward bottom quarter. Direct the ball forcefully to the ground with one hand. The proficient player should be able to bounce the ball with either hand. Try to master all of the following skills (remember to switch hands):

- Bounce the ball with one hand and catch it with both.
- Bounce the ball with one hand and catch it with one.
- Bounce the ball as low to the ground as you can.
- Bounce the ball as close to the ground and as fast as you can.
- Bounce the ball and let it do one complete revolution (backspin) before you catch it.

When you catch the ball, is the seam pointing directly away from you?

These are stationary drills. Complete five bounces with your left hand, giving yourself 1 point for each bounce you are able to catch. Complete five bounces with your right hand, giving yourself 1 point for each bounce you are able to catch. Complete five bounces with your left hand,

making the ball complete one revolution backspin before you catch it. Earn 1 point for each successful bounce and catch. Complete five bounces with your right hand, making the ball complete one revolution backspin before you catch it. Earn 1 point for each successful bounce and catch.

To Increase Difficulty

- Even top players find bouncing with two balls alternately (one with each hand) a challenge to their ball-handling expertise. Try it and work towards mastering it.

Success Check

- Are you comfortable with the bounce?
- Maintain complete control of the ball. It should come back to you and not get away.
- Practise until you are able to use either hand to bounce the ball.

Score Your Success

15 to 20 points = 5 points

10 to 14 points = 3 points

5 to 9 points = 1 point

Your score ____

6

Ball-Handling Drill 7. *Rebound Take*

Throw the ball at various heights against a wall and take the ball on the rebound. At first do it from close range without moving forwards. Gradually increase the distance from the wall and move forwards to take the ball as it rebounds. Try to take the ball in both hands, but failing that, endeavour to prevent the ball from getting past you at all times. As you become more confident, increase the hardness of the throw and the speed at which you approach the ball. Remember: Watch the ball at all times!

Success Check

- Handle the ball confidently with minimum fumbling as you control the ball.
- The ball should not get past you. This is an important fundamental in football.

Score Your Success

Have 25 rebounds. Score 1 point for each successful two-handed take. Take off 3 points if the ball gets past you.

20 to 25 points = 5 points

15 to 19 points = 3 points

10 to 14 points = 1 point

Your score _____

Ball-Handling Drill 8. *Kicking*

The name of the game is *football*, so it's no surprise that players should be continually working on the kicking aspect of their game. A step on kicking is included later in the book, but it is never too early or too late to have a few kicks alone or with someone else to help with ball handling and improving kicking techniques.

Kick back and forth with your partner. Start quite close together and after each kick move slightly farther apart, trying all the time to kick the ball so your partner can catch it on the full. When you are about a maximum (but comfortable) distance apart, try to kick the ball so your partner can catch it without moving more than two or three steps. Don't try to kick from too great a range; accuracy will be affected by trying to kick too hard.

You might like to try a variation. Step forwards three (or more) paces each time your partner can't catch your kick. Step back when he can. See how far apart you get after a certain time.

Success Check

- Practise until you are able to consistently get the ball to your partner.
- Kick for accuracy, not distance.

Score Your Success

At your maximum kicking distance, have 10 kicks each with your partner. Earn 1 point for each successful kick. Come towards your partner several metres and have another 10 kicks each, earning 1 point for each successful kick. Successful kicks are those that your partner can catch.

15 to 20 points = 5 points

10 to 14 points = 3 points

5 to 9 points = 1 point

Your score ___

BALL-HANDLING SUCCESS SUMMARY

Practising and becoming confident in ball handling, whether in handling the ball, kicking it or just having a better understanding of what the ball can do may well be the difference between losing and winning a game or being an average or better player. If you have scored at least 75 points out of 85 in the drills in this step, you are ready to move on. But, as we said at the start of the step, don't ever think you have completely mastered the art of ball handling. Even the best players will still find and learn something by using practice and free time to try different things, analyse them and put themselves to the test. Come back to this step over and over again and devise your own drills and competitions to improve your ball handling.

Ball-Handling Drills

1. Toss and Catch		___ out of 10
2. Hand to Hand		___ out of 10
3. Figure Eights		___ out of 15
4. Bent-Knee Pass		___ out of 15
5. Clenched Fist Punch		___ out of 20
6. Bouncing		___ out of 5
7. Rebound Take		___ out of 5
8. Kicking		___ out of 5
Total		___ **out of 85**

The next step, handballing, is in itself a basic ball-handling skill. For those new to the game, it is somewhat of an unnatural one. It is one of the aspects of our game that make it unique.

Those players who are comfortable in their ball-handling skills, particularly with both hands and on both sides of the body, can make handball a potent footballing weapon.

Handballing

A distinctive feature of Australian football is the disposal of the football with the hands. Unlike in other codes, the ball cannot be thrown or handed off. A player can pass the ball in any direction, and there's no limit to the number of passes that can be made. The rules state, 'A Player shall handball by holding the ball in one hand and hitting it with the clenched fist of the other hand' (15.3).

An obvious way in which football has changed over the last decade or two has been in the use of handballing. The speed of the game, measured primarily by the speed with which the ball moves from player to player up and down the ground, has been greatly attributed to the use of handball and better execution of it.

Previously used primarily as a defensive action when a player was not in a position to kick, handballing has now become a potent offensive weapon. Senior teams handball the ball more than 100 times a game! This feature more than any other has increased the pace of today's game. The play on from a mark or free kick (perhaps more correctly it should be called a free disposal), often with a handball, has meant that the ball rarely stops as the team in possession tries to take advantage of the quick movement and catch the opposition out of position.

Players should not turn and kick blindly downfield, nor should they hold the ball for a long time while getting ready to kick. Teammates should run in the direction of their goals past the player with the ball, who should handball it to them. So, when a player is not in a position to kick effectively and quickly downfield, he will look to handball to a teammate who is.

Like many team games, Australian football is about space. Creating and using space gives the player with the ball time and options when trying to put the ball to advantage. In today's game, handball has many variations, including a long handball to a player in the clear; a shorter, quick handball from a stationary player to a teammate running at speed into space; and a quick, incisive handball from a down-and-under player getting the contested ball out from congested play to a teammate in the clear. Attacking teams must be careful in their execution of handballs: A handball that misses the target or is intercepted will cause a turnover that can be very damaging.

It may seem strange that a book on football deals so early with the skill of handballing. But many of the skill practices presented later for gathering, marking, kicking and so on will involve handballing. Also, handballing is a vital skill and should be learned early, even though it will need modification for youngsters because of the smallness of their hands.

The Birth of the Modern Game

At halftime of the 1970 VFL Grand Final, Carlton, having been completely outplayed and outclassed in every facet of the game, languished 44 points behind Collingwood. With nothing to lose, the iconic player and coach Ron Barassi did not look for match-winning positional moves but instead instructed his players to take risks and to handball and attack their opponents with the run. They did this to perfection, bewildering and exhausting the Magpie players with their innovative 'play on' style; Carlton eventually won the game and the trophy by 10 points. The modern game was born as handball became an attacking rather than defensive weapon in a team's armoury.

This game is also famous for two other reasons. During the game, which was watched by an AFL/VFL record crowd of 121,696, Alex Jesaulenko took what has been described as the 'mark of the century'.

Handballing should become an automatic skill for players. Similarly, players should handball by a reflex action with the appropriate hand as dictated by the take of the ball and the direction of disposal. *Take of the ball* refers to how and where the ball is caught or gathered by the receiving player—high, low, in front of the body or on the side of the body. Ideally the player takes the ball in both hands in front of the body, which offers the best opportunity and options for an immediate dispatch.

Senior coaches demand the 'first give', which means that players need to take possession cleanly in the hands and then almost instan- taneously pass the ball off to a teammate. The first give needs to be second nature because of the necessary speed and because it is the only disposal skill for which the eyes are on the target and not on the ball. Speed, accuracy and an ability to handball from almost any position (even from the ground, although this is not always recommended) with either hand and over a variety of distances—these are the attributes of a skilled, confident handballer. The slow preparation and pass, and the pass with the wrong hand, slows the ball and provides opportunities for interception.

BEGINNING HANDBALL

Footballers are usually advised never to throw a football during practice. Why practise a skill that is not allowed in a game? While performing most of the ball-handling drills, as well as any other activities in this book, handball whenever you can. What follows are some points to remember when practising handballing.

Hold the ball firmly in your hand as shown in figure 2.1. When holding the ball this way, you can move it to any position for handballing. This grip works especially well for players with small hands.

Watch the ball. As you get more proficient, you will watch the target, but at this stage look at the ball, particularly at the spot you are going to punch (figure 2.2a). Punch the ball from the palm of the holding hand (platform hand, figure 2.2b). If you don't do this, you are deemed to be throwing it, which is illegal and in a game results

in a free possession to the opposition. Dropping the ball from the hand is also illegal.

Figure 2.1 Handball grip with support of the lower forearm.

Misstep

Opponents easily knock the ball away or take it from you when you are handballing.

Correction

You are holding the ball too far from your body. Hold it closer with your elbow nearer your body.

Figure 2.2   Beginning Handball

a

b

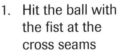

c

PREPARATION

1. Elbow bent
2. Arm cocked
3. Fist formed
4. Platform hand close to the body
5. Watch the ball
6. Head over the ball
7. Grip the ball in the palm

EXECUTION

1. Hit the ball with the fist at the cross seams

FOLLOW-THROUGH

1. Weight on the front foot
2. Punching arm follows through
3. Elbow still bent

Misstep

You drop or throw the ball from your holding hand prior to the hit.

Correction

Hold the ball in your hand and against your wrist. Practise handballing while your holding hand rests on the back of another player who is kneeling. Practise grabbling the wrist of your punching hand with your holding hand after hitting the ball. You will not be able to follow through as far, but your follow-through should still be in a straight line towards the target.

Hit the ball near the back point, where the stitched seams meet. Hit it with the thumb and forefinger area (pad) of your clenched fist. To avoid hurting yourself, be sure to keep your thumb free and not tucked in under your fingers.

Get more power and distance by adding body weight to the handball by stepping forwards towards the target. Step with the foot opposite to the hand that is doing the punching. Follow through with your punching hand upwards and towards the target after it has struck the ball (figure 2.2c).

A way to practise the correct hit is to grab the wrist of your punching hand immediately after hitting the ball. Grab the wrist with the hand that had been holding the ball (figure 2.3).

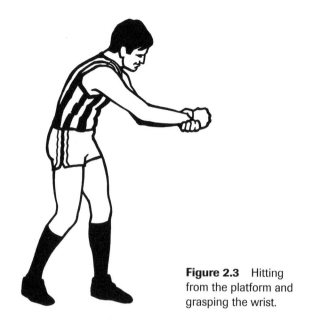

Figure 2.3 Hitting from the platform and grasping the wrist.

TUMBLE HANDBALL

If you sense that you are about to be tackled and have no teammate to give the ball to, you can handball the ball forwards. Punched correctly, the spin of this *tumble pass* will carry it forwards where you can regather it. The tumble pass is also useful to get the ball low past an opponent in front of a teammate. It also tends to bounce higher, making it easier to gather.

For the tumble handball, point the ball in the direction in which you will pass it and hit it just below the junction of the seams at the back of the ball (figure 2.4). As you make contact, relax your grip on the ball slightly, but do not let your hand drop from under the ball. If hit correctly, the ball will spin end over end towards the target.

| Figure 2.4 | Tumble Handball |

PREPARATION

1. Elbow bent
2. Arm cocked
3. Fist formed
4. Platform hand close to the body
5. Watch the target
6. Head over the ball
7. Grip the ball in the palm

a

b

EXECUTION

1. Hit the ball with the fist below the cross seams

Misstep

The handball misses the target.

Correction

Watch the target and not the ball. Turn your head and shoulders to face the target. If passing to a moving player, make sure that the ball is handballed in front of him. Aim at the chest.

The follow-through is identical to the follow-through for the beginning handball. The weight is on your front foot. Follow through with your punching hand, keeping your elbow bent.

Misstep

The umpire interprets the handball as a throw.

Correction

Put the action beyond doubt by always following through with your hitting hand so that the fist finishes in front of the platform hand. Exaggerating this movement can help. When practising, make sure that you can hear your fist hitting the ball.

ROCKET HANDBALL

Senior players will gain more speed, accuracy and distance with their handball by holding the ball at an upwards angle of about 30 degrees and punching it with a firm action just above the back junction of the seams (figure 2.5). This will give a backwards spin to the ball similar to that of a drop-punt kick, making it easier to catch. This is sometimes given the name *rocket handball*.

For the rocket handball, the preparation phase is the same as that for the tumble handball. Watch the target. Hit the ball above the cross seams with your fist. Follow through with your punching arm, keeping your elbow bent. Your weight is on your front foot.

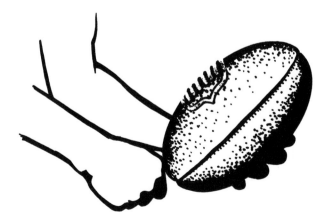

Figure 2.5 For a rocket handball, hit the ball with your fist above the cross seams.

The follow-through for the rocket handball is the same as that for the beginning handball and the tumble handball. Your weight is on your front foot. Follow through with your punching hand, keeping your elbow bent.

HANDBALLING TIPS

The object of the handball is to get the ball to advantage to a teammate. This is best done by delivering the ball in front of the teammate's chest so he can take it in his hands. To achieve this delivery, experienced players watch the target instead of the ball. However, in the early stages of learning (particularly when passing with the nonpreferred hand), players will (and should) watch the ball. Once you have gained confidence and skill in handballing, lift your eyes and look at the target.

To hit the ball with some power, take your elbow back to about shoulder height before striking. Once you have hit the ball, follow through with your punching arm in line with the target. Generally, the elbow is bent at about 90 degrees throughout the punching action. (A straight arm leads to dropping the ball, loss of power and an exaggerated upwards flight of the ball.) Power for distance and speed is generated by stepping towards the target. Do this by stepping with the foot opposite to the hand hitting the ball.

Misstep

You are not able to get much distance or power with the handball.

Correction

Your hitting arm is probably too straight and your fist and wrist not held firmly enough. Bend your elbow, firm up your wrist and punch through the ball. Greater distance and power are achieved with a faster, sharper punch rather than a large back lift with a straight arm. Remember to step towards the target.

The ball should be passed quickly at the first opportunity. The receiver should be calling for the ball, especially when the ball is being picked up from the ground. If there is a call, the ball can be handballed as early as the player hears the call, lifts his eyes and sees the target. He then handballs on the up rather than waiting to stand upright before passing.

The player with the ball still needs to decide whether handballing is to his team's advantage. Generally, the handball is made to either a moving player or a player in a better attacking position. Don't handball for the sake of handballing, particularly to a stationary player who would have to turn to move the ball on towards his goal. Similarly, handballing to a player close to you may not be to advantage particularly if you are trying to avoid a tackle. The receiving player in this case is just as likely to be tackled.

Although taking the ball and handballing over your head or shoulder looks spectacular, it is very risky and likely to be inaccurate. Whenever possible, turn your head, shoulders and the ball towards the target prior to punching.

Equally spectacular but also very risky is handballing while lying on the ground. Because it is difficult to get much power this way and often difficult to get your head and shoulders into position, your handball will likely miss its target (especially when the target player is moving as he should be) or be intercepted. Some coaches make it a rule never to handball from the ground after a mark or a free kick, preferring the player to get up, clear the person standing the mark and either take the kick or play on with a handball to a moving teammate.

As with kicking, when delivering the handball to a moving player, you need to make allowance for that player's speed and movement. Handball the ball in front of the receiver so that he doesn't have to reduce speed or, worse still, have the ball go behind him. If the receiver is coming directly towards you, hit the ball easily enough for him to catch it. In fact, you can lob the ball into the air and the target player's momentum will take him to it.

Right from the start, practise taking the bouncing ball (even the high one for which you have to leap) into your hands and then handballing, rather than batting the ball, in the direction of another player. Again, batting might look spectacular when it comes off, but it is a high-risk, low-percentage technique that should be avoided. Always take the ball and then handball. An exception here is the ruckman, who will immediately be penalised for holding the ball if he takes the ball directly from a bounce or throw-in and is tackled.

Remember that playing conditions affect handballing, as well as other facets of the game. A wet, slippery ball can easily slide off the fist.

In good conditions, handballs of many metres can be made safely and accurately, but when the ball is wet and heavy, you will not be able to achieve the same distances, and you should adjust accordingly. This does not mean that you should not handball at all in the wet, but you will need to take more care. You also need to consider the wind. Just as a punched drop punt will travel farther and more accurately when kicked into the wind, the back-spinning rocket handball is preferred when handballing into the wind, particularly over a distance.

Most errors that occur when handballing are related to dropping the platform hand, making a weak contact with the punching hand or missing the moving target. These and other problems can be overcome by a return to the fundamentals of handballing.

Handballing Drill 1. *Target Ball*

Practise handballing the ball against a wall and try to take it cleanly as it rebounds. Vary the distance from the wall and be sure to practise with both hands. With chalk draw five boxes about 30 centimetres square at various heights on the wall. Draw a line four steps from the wall (figure 2.6). Standing behind the line, see how many passes it takes to hit every box in order twice (10 boxes in all). Do not move to box 2 until you have hit box 1 once and so on. After every pass move quickly to recover the ball and return behind your restraining line for the next shot. Be sure to turn your head and shoulders towards the target each time. Have five attempts.

To Increase Difficulty

- Make the boxes smaller or have the restraining line farther away. You may also set a time limit to speed up the handballing.

Success Check

- Make clean contact with the thumb and forefinger pad on the ball.
- Step towards the target with the foot opposite the punching hand.
- Follow through with your fist.
- Don't drop the ball!

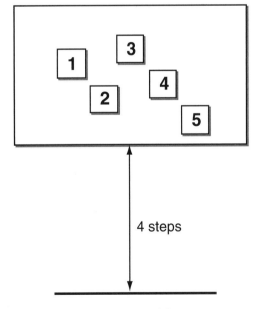

Figure 2.6 Setup for target-ball drill.

Score Your Success

Hit all 10 boxes in 10 handballs = 10 points

Hit all 10 boxes in 11 to 15 handballs = 5 points

Hit all 10 boxes in 16 to 20 handballs = 1 point

Your score ___

Handballing Drill 2.   *Put It in a Bin*

This drill is similar to drill 1, but this time instead of a target on the wall use a rubbish bin in the middle of a circle 7 to 10 metres in diameter (figure 2.7). Put some rocks into the bin so it doesn't topple. Always recover the ball and go outside the circle to handball. Have 25 shots.

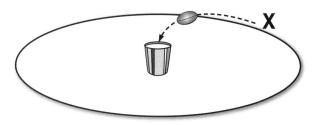

Figure 2.7   Setup for put-it-in-a-bin drill.

To Increase Difficulty

• Enlarge the restraining circle.

Success Check

• Give the ball a little more 'air' to lob it into the bin.
• Square your head and shoulders to the target.
• Watch the target.

Score Your Success

20 to 25 bins out of 25 shots = 5 points

15 to 19 bins out of 25 shots = 3 points

10 to 14 bins out of 25 shots = 1 point

Your score ___

Handballing Drill 3.   *Line Ball*

This drill is designed specifically to practise the tumble pass and to develop power in the handball. Draw two lines 20 metres apart. Stand behind one line and use the tumble pass to handball towards the far line (figure 2.8). Chase after the ball and pick it up once it has stopped rolling or gone over the line. Count 1 if the ball goes over the line; if it doesn't go over the line, it doesn't count. Repeat after coming back to the starting line. How many tries does it take to get 10? Alternate punching hands.

Figure 2.8   Setup for line-ball drill.

To Increase Difficulty

• Do this drill with a friend. Turn the drill into a race.

Success Check

• Step forwards as you handball.
• Exaggerate your follow-through.
• Do not allow the holding hand to drop the ball as you strive for distance.

Score Your Success

Need 10 handballs to score 10 = 5 points

Need 11 or 12 handballs to score 10 = 3 points

Need 13 or 14 handballs to score 10 = 1 point

Your score ___

Handballing Drill 4. *Partner Target Ball*

Using the box targets and restraining line you used in handballing drill 1, have alternate shots at the targets with your partner. The player who handballs at the target recovers the ball and then handballs back to the other, who is standing behind the restraining line. Each box is to be hit in turn (1 to 5 and then 5 to 1). Count the number of shots it takes to successfully make 10 hits.

To Increase Difficulty

- Make the drill competitive by going against your partner. The player who gets 10 hits in the fewest number of attempts wins.

Success Check

- Sprint after handballing the ball and gather it cleanly.
- Once you have recovered the ball, turn to face your partner, becoming square on to him before handballing.

Score Your Success

Hit all 10 boxes in 10 handballs = 5 points

Hit all 10 boxes in 11 to 15 handballs = 3 points

Hit all 10 boxes in 16 to 20 handballs = 1 point

Your score ___

Handballing Drill 5. *Two-Ball Handball*

Three players form a triangle (figure 2.9). Players A and B each have a ball and alternately handball to player C, who has to take the ball and handball back to the person who gave it to him. Count the number of handballs player C makes in a minute. Take turns so that each player has a chance to receive.

Success Check

- Take the ball cleanly and turn slightly to the target before handballing.
- When handballing to your left, use your right hand. When handballing to your right, use your left hand.

Score Your Success

Complete 45 to 50 handballs = 5 points

Complete 40 to 44 handballs = 3 points

Complete 35 to 39 handballs = 1 point

Your score ___

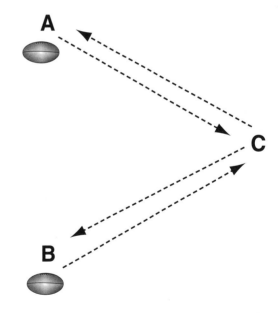

Figure 2.9 Setup for two-ball handball drill.

Handballing Drill 6. *Keep the Ball Away*

In a group of four, play 'keep the ball away' in pairs in a 10-metre-square area (figure 2.10). A goal is scored by hitting a cone or a post or by handballing into a bin. After a missed shot, the opponents get the ball outside the square. This is a noncontact game without any tackling. The ball is obtained by intercepting the opponent's handball.

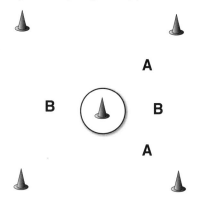

Figure 2.10 Setup for keep-the-ball-away drill.

Other than one or two steps to break clear, there should be no running with the ball.

Success Check

- Move to be in a clear position to receive the ball.
- Handball to your partner in a position in which he can take it with minimal chance for interception.
- Always try to square your shoulders and hips towards your target, be it your partner or the scoring target.
- Handball using the correct hand.

Score Your Success

Score more goals than your opponents in a five-minute game = 5 points

Your score ___

Handballing Drill 7. *Pig in the Middle*

Mark a 5-metre square. Three players are in three of the corners and one player is in the middle of the square (figure 2.11). The ball can be passed to the corners only down the sides, not across the square. The object is to keep the ball away from the middle player. The outside players may (should) move to the vacant corner of the square to take the ball. Change the middle player when the ball

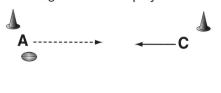

Figure 2.11 Setup for pig-in-the-middle drill.

is intercepted or after a set time. Earn 5 points if none of your handballs are intercepted by the pig in the middle. When you are the pig in the middle, earn 1 point for each handball you intercept.

To Increase Difficulty

- Have a larger square.

Success Check

- Use accurate, sharp hand passes to avoid interceptions.
- Handball to the spot where the player will move.
- Be prepared to move quickly to the spare cone to give a second option for the player with the ball.

Score Your Success

5 points or more = 10 points

Your score ___

HANDBALLING ON THE OVAL

With each of the team drills, and indeed most of the others in the book, the lines should not be so long that players are standing about waiting their turns. Maximum involvement will give greater opportunity to practise the skills involved. This will of necessity mean that more footballs may well be needed. Conversely, teams should not be so small that players tire quickly and technique suffers. Distances should be made appropriate to the age and size of the players.

Each of the drills can be made more difficult as technique improves by adding more pressure by increasing the speed of the ball or players, adding a competitive element and perhaps requiring players to make decisions by providing options within the drill.

An important factor quite often forgotten is that the player receiving the handball has the responsibility of getting into the right position to do so. Whenever possible, the handball should go to a moving player. That moving player should be easily visible to the player with the ball so that the player can execute a successful handball. For the following drills, emphasis should be not only on the handpass itself but also on the moving player positioning himself to take the ball at an advantage.

Misstep

You always use your dominant hand to handpass.

Correction

When the receiving player is to your left, hit the ball with your right hand. When the receiving player is to your right, hit the ball with your left hand.

More team drills involving handpassing are included in steps that follow. Also, the following handball team drills may well be adapted and used as kicking drills.

Team Handballing Drill 1. *Shuttle Handball*

This is the traditional simple team handball drill. Player A runs towards player B, handballs to him and follows through to the end of the line. Player B handballs to player C, and so on. For variety, include putting or rolling the ball on the ground at one end to practise handballing on the up, handballing above the head from one end to encourage leaping to take the ball and recovering and then handballing to the oncoming player. Players should be encouraged to vary their approach to the oncoming player so as to practise taking the ball and handpassing from both sides and using both left and right hands for the handpass.

To Increase Difficulty

- Place one or more players between the end groups so that the players running through have to take and dispose of the ball several times and preferably with alternate hands.

Success Check

- Work on giving and receiving handballs while on the move.

- Gather the ball from the ground and handball it accurately.

- Handball using the appropriate hand.

Team Handballing Drill 2. *Pepper Ball*

Pepper ball is an extension of shuttle handball. It requires a number of footballs and players who are proficient in taking and handpassing the ball.

Players in teams A and C have a ball each. They run through to the opposite end handballing to the players in team B, timing their runs so that each player in team B has to take and give the ball from alternate sides (figure 2.12). After several run-throughs, team A takes its turn in the middle, and then team C does.

To Increase Difficulty

- As players become more efficient, vary the predictability of the exercise by having the run-through teams randomly weave through the stationary team.

Success Check

- Watch the ball into your hands each time you receive the ball.
- Take the ball in your hands.
- Handball with the correct hand—the left hand when handballing to the right and vice versa.
- Don't make it an effort for the person receiving your handball to catch it.

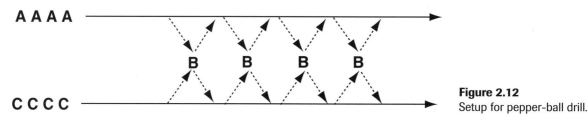

Figure 2.12
Setup for pepper-ball drill.

Team Handballing Drill 3. *Crossover*

Player A runs towards player B (who is moving towards him), handpasses to player B and goes to the end of the B line (figure 2.13). Player B takes the ball and handpasses to player C, who is running towards player D. Player C handpasses to player D, who handpasses to player A and so on. After handpassing the ball, each player goes to the end of the line from which the receiving player came.

Success Check

- Watch the ball into your hands.
- Handball with the correct hand.
- Handball the ball in front of the receiving player to allow him to run into it and not to have to stop or break stride.
- Feel comfortable ball handling in a confined area with other players about.

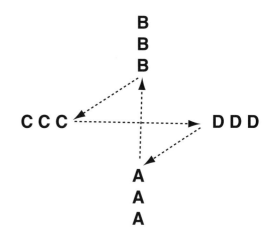

Figure 2.13 Setup for crossover drill.

Team Handballing Drill 4. *Three-Man Weave*

Player A handpasses to player B, who has run in front of him (figure 2.14). Player B gives to player C and player C gives back to player A as they crisscross until the ball is handpassed to player D, who gives to player E and so on. Each player has to run wide and fast enough to ensure that the ball is always handpassed forwards.

Success Check

- The ball is given and taken by players on the move and at some speed.
- The ball is handballed forwards.
- Players run hard to be in position to receive the ball.

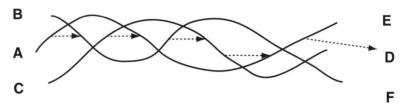

Figure 2.14 Setup for three-man-weave drill.

Team Handballing Drill 5. *Grid Handball*

Player A begins the drill. The ball is worked around the grid using handball (figure 2.15). Each player follows his handball to the next group. To challenge the players further, the coach can add more footballs at his discretion and enlarge the grid to lengthen the required handballs.

Success Check

- Handball to in front of the waist of the receiving player.

- Handball crisply with a definite punch on the ball.

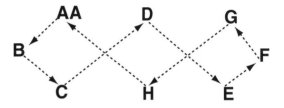

Figure 2.15 Setup for grid-handball drill.

Team Handballing Drill 6. *Follow-Up Handball*

Player A starts with the ball and handballs into the middle to player B, who receives and passes to player C (figure 2.16). Player C handballs down the line to player D, who gives a handball back in the middle to player E. Player E handballs to player F, who handballs down the line to group A. Players must follow the ball to the group they have handballed to.

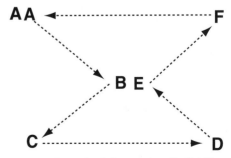

Figure 2.16 Setup for follow-up handball drill.

Success Check

- Give the ball sufficient elevation for the distance the ball will have to travel.
- With the long handball, take several running steps towards the receiving player.

- Attempt to get every handball to the player on the full.
- Follow your handball by running quickly to the next position.

Team Handballing Drill 7. *Handball and Shoot*

Two teams start about 25 to 30 metres from goals in a crisscross formation. Each team has a football. Each team handballs in a shuttle manner in a straight line with players handballing and following through to the end of the team. The coach randomly blows a whistle and the person with the ball at that time has to snap at goal. Scores are recorded, and after several turns there is a penalty for the losing side.

Here is a variation to try: On the whistle, if the player with the ball is facing away from goals, he handballs to an alert teammate who has the shot at goal.

Success Check

- Do not make it difficult for your approaching teammate by handballing too hard.
- Do this drill at game speed.
- If you have to kick, make sure you kick high at the goals to get over the players.

HANDBALLING SUCCESS SUMMARY

You now have had a chance to understand and practise the skill of handballing. However, you have just begun to understand and appreciate the role that handballing can play in a game. As you move on to other steps and do the skills and drills there, don't assume that you have learned all there is to learn about handballing. Good players are able to handball prodigious distances at times with either hand. As the speed of their reflex give increases, so does their ability not only to get out of tight game situations but also to set up team attacking plays.

Continue to work on this basic football skill. Make it a practice never to throw the football and to always handball with the appropriate hand. In games so many turnovers occur from misdirected handpasses or just poor handpassing techniques that fall apart under the pressure of a game.

Handballing Drills	
1. Target Ball	___ out of 10
2. Put It in a Bin	___ out of 5
3. Line Ball	___ out of 5
4. Partner Target Ball	___ out of 5
5. Two-Ball Handball	___ out of 5
6. Keep the Ball Away	___ out of 5
7. Pig in the Middle	___ out of 10
Total	___ *out of 45*

If you scored more than 35 points out of 45, you have shown that you have enough handballing skill to move on to the next step. But remember to keep returning to the success check points to improve and extend your handballing skills. Before you can handball the ball, however, you need to have it in your possession. That is what the next step, gathering the ball, is all about.

Gathering the Ball

Before you can dispose of the ball, either by handballing (step 2) or kicking (step 5), you must first possess the ball. One of the highlights of Australian football is that players contest the ball fiercely, whether the ball is in the air or on the ground. By constantly watching the ball and being confident in your ability to handle and read the ball, you will take the strong positive approach necessary in taking the ball ahead of your opponent. You develop the ability to read the ball by practising getting into the position to gather the ball on the ground, mark the kicked ball or take the handballed, bouncing or falling ball.

In a typical senior game more than 400 kicks could be marked, allowing an uncontested kick to be taken. However, normally less than a third of kicked balls are marked. Marking is difficult; competition for possession is fierce, and conditions are often adverse. More often than not, the ball is not marked, and it comes to ground. In some situations the ball cannot be marked and is deliberately brought to ground, such as in ruck contests from a bounce or a throw-in or in a deliberate set play, spoiling the ball or knocking it on.

GATHERING THE LOOSE BALL

A common method of taking possession during a game is by gathering a loose ball, a ball that is free on the ground. The ball is most likely to be stationary in junior football because it is often kicked well clear of players and has time to come to a stop before players get to it. In senior games, the ball is going to be kicked or knocked with more accuracy and will rarely be so much in the clear that it will come to a complete stop. Senior players will also be quicker than junior players to get to the ball. Whether the ball is

stationary on the ground (figure 3.1) or moving (figure 3.2), follow these fundamentals to gather the ball from the ground.

Approach the ball confidently. Expect to pick it up. Keep your eyes on the ball as you take it into your hands or body.

Keep your body behind the ball and your head above the ball. If you are unable to take the ball in your hands, your arms and body following should block its movement past you and keep it in front. Approaching the ball from an indirect line does not allow for maximum coverage of a bounce to either side, nor does an approach from the side with a thrust of one arm out to take the ball.

Bend from the hips *and* the knees to get down to the ball. This ensures that you are better balanced, less likely to stumble and in a better position to withstand a bump or a tackle from an opponent. Also, if the ball stays low or skids, you are better positioned to cover it if you are crouched. It is easier to quickly come out of a crouch if the ball bounces higher than it is to stoop quickly to cover a low ball.

The half-volley take (taking the ball into the hands as it hits the ground) is most effective for taking the bouncing ball because it eliminates the uncertainties of the bounce. The higher the take, the more variation of direction is possible.

Take the ball with the palms facing it, fingers spread, arms slightly bent, and elbows tucked into the body to provide a pocket into which the ball can go if necessary. Young players particularly should try to get the ball into this pocket. As your skill and confidence develop, you should try to take the ball in your hands to provide more time for effective disposal. Do not snatch at the ball.

Figure 3.1   Gathering a Stationary Ball on the Ground

a   b   c

PREPARATION

1. Body in line with the ball
2. Head over the ball
3. Cupped hands and fingers behind the ball with fingers pointing to the ground
4. Arms and hands extended
5. Arms cradled and chest hollowed
6. Elbows tucked to the sides
7. Knees bent
8. Hips bent

EXECUTION

1. Ball taken in the hands
2. Head over the ball

FOLLOW-THROUGH

1. Ball ready to be handballed or kicked

Misstep

You are easily pushed off the ball.

Correction

In a game situation, if you are about to be bumped, it is even more vital to get your body low and over the ball by bending at the knees and hips. If you are about to be bumped as you pick up the ball, spread your feet a little and lean into the bumping player, keeping your elbows close to your body and scooping the ball onto your chest.

| Figure 3.2 | **Gathering a Bouncing Ball** |

a

b

c

PREPARATION

1. Body in line with the ball
2. Head over the ball
3. Cupped hands and fingers behind the ball with fingers pointing to the ground
4. Arms and hands extended
5. Arms cradled and chest hollowed
6. Elbows tucked to the sides
7. Knees and hips bent if the bounce is low

EXECUTION

1. Ball taken in the hands

FOLLOW-THROUGH

1. Ball ready to be hand-balled or kicked

Misstep

You overrun, miss or fumble the ball when you try to gather it as it bounces on the ground.

Correction

If the ball is bouncing erratically, be ready to adjust and take it in your hands. Wait until you have the ball in your control before you take your eyes off it to look where you are going to deliver it.

Because of the ball's shape, it can bounce any which way. However, we know that certain circumstances will lead to certain types of bounce.

If the ground and the ball are wet, the ball will hit and skid. When this occurs, your body should act as a backstop to the ball. Your first choice will be to take the ball on your chest, very much like a low chest mark. As the ball bounces into your chest, wrap your arms around the ball with your elbows close together, hugging the ball to your chest while supporting the ball underneath, in front and over it.

If the ground is particularly muddy, the ball will tend to stop suddenly and stick. In such cases you need to bend low and get your hands and forearms behind and under the ball.

On firm ground the ball will bounce higher, and good judgment is required to pick the angle,

trajectory and height of the bounce. Make necessary adjustments to your speed and direction to take possession.

If the ball is bouncing *towards* you, you can generally attack more confidently with your hands and arms acting as a scoop. If your approach to the ball is direct, you can easily make adjustments for bounce.

If the ball is bouncing *away* from you, your approach should be a little more cautious. You might be tempted to knock the ball forwards for a more favourable bounce, but this is discouraged. There is also a tendency to bend from the hips only, which might make you stumble over the ball. An approach slightly to the side of the ball with knees bent and head over the ball is better.

A good practice to develop early is to always take the ball and then handball or kick, rather than knock on the bouncing ball. This practice will lead to better, quicker and more accurate disposal, particularly for the high-bouncing ball.

All players need to know the rule about holding the ball. Once you have gathered the ball, you have a reasonable time (as judged by the umpire) to dispose of it. You must attempt to do this when tackled. If both you and the ball are on the ground, it may be safer to knock the ball on (figure 3.3) or hit it towards a teammate. Certainly, you should not pull the ball back towards or under yourself as you are tackled.

In knocking or hitting on, you do not attempt to gather the ball, but hit it, usually with an open hand, into the path of a teammate who is better placed to pick it up and dispose of it. Take care not to scoop the ball up or momentarily hold it, as the subsequent disposal will then be judged a throw, and a free kick will be awarded to the opposition.

Figure 3.3 Knocking the ball on.

Desperate Times Require Desperate Means

Late in the 1979 Carlton–Collingwood Grand Final, Carlton's Wayne Harmes chased the ball towards the boundary. The ball was wet and slippery and the ground was muddy. Harmes dove and slid in the mud after the ball, hitting it just before it crossed the line. He knocked it with his hand into the path of his teammate Ken Sheldon as Sheldon raced into goal. Sheldon gathered the ball cleanly and kicked it through the goals, giving Carlton a 10-point break late in the game. They were able to hold on for an eventual 5-point win.

Most ball-handling errors in gathering have two causes: not getting down to the ball or taking your eyes off the ball. You should bend at both the knees and the hips to get your arms and body to act like a scoop behind the ball. It is also vital that you watch the ball.

Misstep

You knock the ball ahead and wait for a favourable bounce before taking the ball.

Correction

Go confidently for the ball. Bend low to scoop it up. Do not snatch at the ball. Get in position early and try to take the ball on the half volley as it bounces.

Gathering-the-Ball Drill 1. *Stationary Ball*

Practise picking up a stationary ball. Handball the ball a few metres away from you. Wait until it has stopped. Chase after the ball and pick it up. Do this 15 times, alternating handballing directly in front of you and 45 degrees to your left and 45 degrees to your right. Earn 1 point each time you gather the ball cleanly without fumbling it.

To Increase Difficulty

- Have a player or coach move to near the ball and make a token effort to bump the player who is picking up the ball.

Success Check

- How comfortable are you with gathering a stationary ball?
- Did you have your head over the ball?
- Bending your knees will give you a better balance to pick up the ball.
- Score only clean gathers in which you do not fumble the ball at all.

Score Your Success

15 out of 15 points = 5 points

14 out of 15 points = 3 points

13 out of 15 points = 1 point

Your score ＿＿

Gathering-the-Ball Drill 2. *Oncoming Bouncing*

From 5 to 10 metres away, throw the ball against a wall at about waist height and move forwards to gather it up as it rebounds. Because of the shape of the ball, it could well bounce back in the air. If this occurs, try to catch it and make sure it does not get past you. Complete 25 rebounds.

To Increase Difficulty

- Start closer to the wall and throw the ball harder at the wall. This will give you less time to judge and take the rebounding ball.

Success Check

- Move forwards to take the ball either on the ground or in the air. Don't wait for it to come to you.
- Watch the ball.
- If you didn't take the ball cleanly, were you able to stop it getting past you?

Score Your Success

23 to 25 rebounds gathered = 5 points

20 to 22 rebounds gathered = 3 points

17 to 19 rebounds gathered = 1 point

Your score ＿＿

Gathering-the-Ball Drill 3.   *Roll Retrieval*

Roll the ball away from you and chase after it. Chase after it hard and pick it up while it is still moving. Do this 15 times. If you get to the ball after it stops, it does not count as 1 of your 15 tries.

Success Check

- Score only if you gather the ball cleanly and without fumbling.
- Attack the ball—don't wait for the ball to slow down.
- Have your hands and fingers relaxed to take the ball.

Score Your Success

Give yourself 1 point for each ball you successfully gather in your hands. If you fumble or take the ball on your chest, no points are scored.

15 out of 15 points = 5 points

14 out of 15 points = 3 points

13 out of 15 points = 1 point

Your score ___

Gathering-the-Ball Drill 4.   *Gather and Shoot*

For this drill you will essentially repeat the first three drills but with a target. Place the target at about waist height.

First, practise gathering a stationary ball, as in drill 1. Place the ball on the ground about 10 metres from the wall. Run from about 15 metres from the wall and pick up the ball. Once you have gathered the ball, handball it from about 5 metres to hit the target on the wall. Practise from both sides of the target so that you have to use both hands when handballing. Make five attempts from each side.

Next, practise gathering the ball off a rebound, as in drill 2. From about 10 to 15 metres away, roll the ball hard at the wall. Run towards the rebounding ball. Gather it as quickly as possible off the rebound and handball it to hit the target. Make five attempts from each side.

Finally, from about 15 metres roll a ball along the ground and gather it before it comes to a stop,

as in the second part of drill 3. After gathering the ball, handball it to hit the target. Gather and handball from both sides of the target. Make five attempts from each side.

Success Check

- Try to gather the ball cleanly and hit the target with each attempt.
- Watch the ball and bend your knees.
- Handball with the correct hand.

Score Your Success

Hit the target 25 to 30 times = 5 points

Hit the target 20 to 24 times = 3 points

Hit the target 10 to 19 times = 1 point

Your score ___

Gathering-the-Ball Drill 5.   *Roller Ball*

Compete with a partner to see who is able to gather cleanly the most often. From about 10 metres roll the ball to your partner, who comes forwards to trap, control and gather the ball and handball it back. Gradually increase the speed and difficulty of the bounce for your partner.

Your partner receives 1 point each time he takes the ball cleanly, but loses 3 points whenever the handball back is not catchable. Have five turns and then change roles. Change twice more so that each player has 10 attempts to gather and handball.

Success Check

- Keep your eyes on the ball.
- Gather the ball cleanly.
- This is a competitive drill. Try to score more points than your partner.
- Handball accurately.

Score Your Success

Score more points than your partner = 5 points

Score fewer points than your partner = 0 points

Your score ___

Gathering-the-Ball Drill 6.   *Shin Ball*

Stand four steps away from a partner and handball the ball at your partner's feet, which are shoulder-width apart. Your partner has to bend and control the ball, pick it up and handball it back to you. Change over after every 10 handballs. Add difficulty by handballing to the middle or either side of your partner's legs. Score 3 points for getting the ball between your partner's legs, 2 for hitting his legs, or 1 if he fumbles the take.

Success Check

- Keep your knees and hips bent for better balance.

- Keep your hands and arms in a ready position to take the ball.
- This is a competitive drill. Try to score more points than your partner.

Score Your Success

Score more points than your partner = 5 points

Score fewer points than your partner = 0 points

Your score ___

Gathering-the-Ball Drill 7.   *Ball Chase and Gather*

Stand beside a partner, who rolls the ball away from you. Chase the ball, pick it up and handball back to your partner. Your partner rolls it back towards you so you can pick it up as you return to your starting position. Change over and have 10 turns each for a total of 20 gathers and 20 handballs. Give yourself a point for each successful gather and each successful handball. Lose a point for each fumble or uncatchable handball.

Success Check

- Try to gather the ball and handball it 20 times without error.

Score Your Success

30 to 40 points = 5 points

20 to 29 points = 3 points

10 to 19 points = 1 point

Your score ___

Gathering-the-Ball Drill 8.   *Gather the Bouncing Ball*

In groups of no more than six, players will practise gathering balls bouncing away from them as well as ones oncoming. Players stand in a row 15 metres apart from each other. Player A rolls the ball towards player B, who gathers and handballs back to player A. Player A then rolls the ball away from player B, who gathers and handballs to player C, who runs up to take the place of player A. Player A goes to the end of the line. Continue until each player has 10 run-throughs (20 attempts to gather). Figure 3.4 shows the drill with four players.

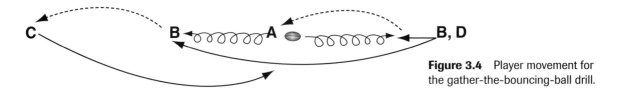

Figure 3.4 Player movement for the gather-the-bouncing-ball drill.

Success Check

- Try to gather the ball 20 times without fumbling.

Gathering-the-Ball Drill 9. *Gather the Angled Bouncing Ball*

Do drill 8 again but this time roll the ball to either side of the gathering player. Players stand in a row 15 metres apart. Player A rolls the ball to the side of player B, who gathers and handballs back to player A. Player A then rolls the ball away from player B, who gathers and handballs to player C, who runs up to take the place of player A. Player A goes to the end of the line. Continue until each player has 10 run-throughs (20 attempts to gather).

Success Check

- Try to gather the ball 20 times without fumbling.
- Watch the ball into your hands and then lift your eyes to see the target for your handball.
- Have soft hands so that the ball doesn't bounce off them.

Gathering-the-Ball Drill 10. *Half-Volley Take*

Have a partner or coach lob the ball to bounce in front of you as you advance towards it. Attempt to take the ball on the half volley or, failing that, prevent the ball from getting past by covering the bounce with your arms and body. Score 3 points for taking the ball cleanly or 1 point for keeping the ball in front of you. Take off 2 points if the ball gets past you. Repeat 10 times.

Success Check

- Keep the ball in front of you.
- Block the ball with your body.

Gathering-the-Ball Drill 11. *Defend the Target*

Play with six players using one ball. One player defends two cones from five players in a circle with a 2-metre radius (figure 3.5). The cones should be 50 centimetres apart. The defender may not go between or leap or reach over the cones. The surrounding players roll the ball at the cones and can handball the ball to a better position among themselves. Each player defends the cones for one minute. The defender loses 1 point every time a cone is hit, but gets 5 points every time he takes the ball cleanly. After gathering the ball, the defender knocks or handballs it back to the surrounding players.

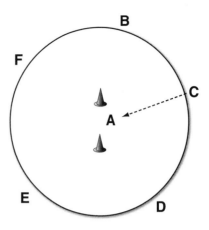

Figure 3.5 Setup for defend-the-target drill.

Success Check

- Watch the ball as it is handballed between players.
- Move into position early to defend the cones.
- Keep your knees and hips bent and your body low for balance when gathering the ball.

Score Your Success

Score at least 25 points in one minute = 5 points

Score 20 to 24 points in one minute = 3 points

Score 15 to 19 points in one minute = 1 point

Your score ___

Gathering-the-Ball Drill 12. *Barrier Ball*

Players A, B and C stand in a row about 10 metres away from player D. Player D rolls, bounces, kicks or lobs the ball quite awkwardly in front of the three advancing players (players A, B and C), whose objective is to prevent the ball getting past them (figure 3.6). Players A, B and C call to the best-positioned player to gather the ball. After gathering the ball, the called player immediately handballs to one of the other players. That player handballs to the third player, who relays the ball back to player D. Player D gets 1 point if the ball gets behind all three of the oncoming players. Players A, B and C get 1 point each if they are able to keep the ball in front of the group.

Figure 3.6 Setup for barrier-ball drill.

Success Check

- The ball is not to get behind the barrier.
- Handballs are to be accurate.
- The three players in the barrier all are moving forwards towards the ball.

Score Your Success

As player D, you score more than players A, B and C = 5 points

As player D, you score less than players A, B and C = 0 points

As player A, B or C, you score more than player D = 5 points

As player A, B or C, you score less than player D = 0 points

Your score ___

Gathering-the-Ball Drill 13. *Team Crossover*

A number of the team drills in the handball step—the crossover drill (page 20), for example—can be modified to be used to practise gathering the ball. In using these drills, players should be encouraged to gather the ball cleanly and then handball to the next player, who will roll or bounce the ball to the next group.

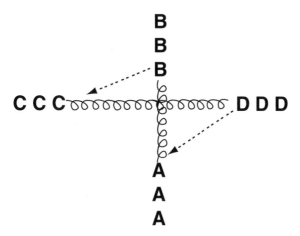

Figure 3.7 Setup for team crossover drill.

Player A runs towards player B (who is moving towards player A), rolls the ball towards player B and goes to the end of player B's line (figure 3.7). Player B takes the ball and handpasses to player C, who is running towards player D. Player C rolls the ball to player D, who gathers the ball and handballs to the next player A. After handpassing or rolling the ball, the player goes to the end of the line from which the receiving player came.

To Increase Difficulty

- Roll the ball at an angle from player B to player C and from player D to player A.

Success Check

- Players do not wait for the ball but move confidently towards it to gather it on the move.
- Handballs are accurate and in a position where the receiving player does not have to slow down to take them cleanly.

GATHERING THE BALL OFF HANDS OR OFF THE PACK

A group of players leaping to contest for a ball in the air is called a *pack*. If the ball is not caught and falls from the contesting play, it is said to be *off hands* or *off the pack*. Defensive players often will not attempt to catch the ball but will block their opponent's attempt by punching the ball. This is called *spoiling* (see step 9) and results in the ball falling off hands. An important skill is to be able to read and take the ball off hands. This skill is practised whenever marking (see step 4) is practised in groups.

To successfully gather the ball off hands, begin by watching the ball (figure 3.8a). Judge the flight of the ball and the positions of the play-ers before positioning yourself. A ball kicked into the wind will drop short, so the best position is to the front of the pack. A ball kicked with the wind will carry, so the best position is to the side of the pack to enable you to go either forwards or backwards.

Time your move so that you don't move too early and are past the ball or too late and have the ball intercepted by an opponent. Watch the ball come off hands right into your hands. Take the ball in both hands as in marking (figure 3.8b). After gathering the ball off hands, get rid of it by handballing or kicking it (figure 3.8c).

Figure 3.8   Taking the Ball Off Hands

PREPARATION

1. Eyes on the ball
2. Get in the best position
3. Be on the move
4. Hands ready to take the ball
5. Fingers spread
6. Don't snatch at the ball

a

b

c

EXECUTION

1. Watch the ball
2. Take the ball in both hands

FOLLOW-THROUGH

1. Move away from the pack to kick or handball
2. Dispose of the ball by handball or kick

When positioning to gather off hands, you need to be either close to the competing players to gather the ball as it drops from the hands or 4 or 5 metres from them to gather the ball as it is spoiled by a defender by punching away (figure 3.9).

The term *front and square* is often used to describe the best positioning for the player to gather the ball off hands. That is, in front of the competing pack and square on to it ready to move in either direction to take the spilled ball.

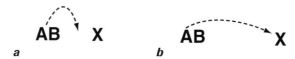

Figure 3.9   To gather from a spoil, *(a)* be close to gather off hands or *(b)* be a few metres away to gather a ball spoiled by a defender punching away.

Gathering-the-Ball-Off-Hands Drill 1. *Six-Player Drill*

Player D kicks the ball high for players B and C to compete for it in the air. Player A positions himself front and square (the ball should ideally pass directly over his head) to read the ball off hands and gather it cleanly. As player A takes the ball, players B and C move past him and call for a handball. Player A kicks the ball high for players E and F to compete for it in the air. Player D takes the ball off hands. Players rotate their positions in their group so that all take turns to read the ball off hands.

To Increase Difficulty

- Vary the height and distance of the incoming ball.
- Have the ball coming in from varying angles so that the player has to move more to get into correct position to judge and take the ball.
- Have groups of four so that there is an element of competition going for the ball both in the air and on the ground.

To Decrease Difficulty

- Have a coach or player lob the ball into the air from a short distance for the competing players.
- Nominate which player is to try to mark the ball with the other player spoiling.

Success Check

- Watch the ball in flight, off hands and into your hands.
- Move into position early to be balanced and have feet slightly spread to change position to take the ball.
- The player who is to take the ball off hands should be front and square.

he-Ball-Off-Hands Drill 2. *Team Drill*

or the two players in group
all in the air (figure 3.10).
ıp B come in with the ball
nds and work together by
ng to get into position to
e two players in group C,
l, with the players in group
ball off hands. One of the
the ball to the next group
of players in group A. Players move to the next
group after each effort: Group A becomes group
B, group B becomes group C, group C becomes
group D, and group D becomes group A.

This drill can be modified by having a coach
kick the ball high for the players in group A to
compete for in the air (figure 3.11). The players
in group B take the ball off hands and kick to
the players in group C, who compete for the ball.
When group D takes the ball off hands, they have
a snap shot at goal.

More off-hands drills will be included in team
drills in later steps.

Success Check

- Watch the ball in flight, off hands and into
  your hands.

- Move into position early to be balanced and
  have feet slightly spread to change position
  to take the ball and have a shot at goal.

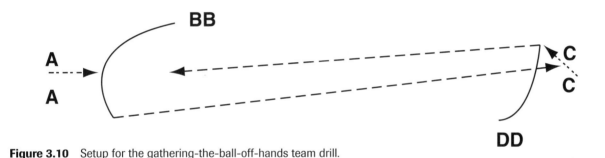

Figure 3.10 Setup for the gathering-the-ball-off-hands team drill.

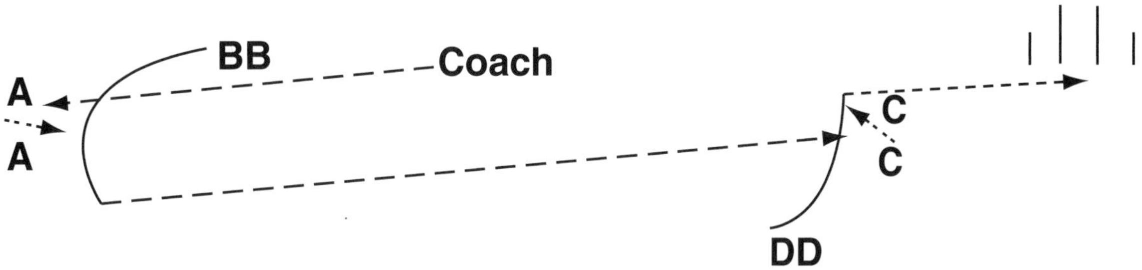

Figure 3.11 Off-hands team drill modification in which a coach kicks the ball high to the players in group A.

GATHERING-THE-BALL SUCCESS SUMMARY

If in the gathering step you have just completed you scored 50 or more out of 65, you have shown that you are comfortable in handling the ball on the ground. Now move on to taking it in the air.

Gathering-the-Ball Drills

1. Stationary Ball	___ out of 5	
2. Oncoming Bouncing	___ out of 5	
3. Roll Retrieval	___ out of 5	
4. Gather and Shoot	___ out of 5	
5. Roller Ball	___ out of 5	
6. Shin Ball	___ out of 5	
7. Ball Chase and Gather	___ out of 5	
8. Gather the Bouncing Ball	___ out of 5	
9. Gather the Angled Bouncing Ball	___ out of 5	
10. Half-Volley Take	___ out of 5	
11. Defend the Target	___ out of 5	
12. Barrier Ball	___ out of 10	
Total	**___ out of 65**	

Taking the ball when it is on the ground is only one way to take possession of the ball. When the ball has been kicked in the air, taking the ball on the full is the preferred option. This is called marking, which is the next step.

Marking

Nothing captures the excitement of Australian football better than the soaring mark, in which a player leaps high over opponents and teammates to grab the ball. This is the most spectacular form of mark, but the chest mark is no less important in a game or as a first step for juniors in learning. Good players know when to use what type of mark.

A *mark* is catching the ball directly from the kick of another player who is no less than 15 metres distant, the ball not having been touched while in transit from kick to catch. Once having marked the ball, the player is entitled to a free kick without interference from an opponent unless he elects to play on by kick, handpass or run.

Kicking a ball to a stationary player is generally discouraged because the ball is easily defended against and often intercepted. Therefore a player will attempt to kick the ball so it will meet a teammate who is moving away from his opponent. The moving player is said to be leading or making a lead.

A mark gives the player the option of either continuing on playing in a contested fashion or taking his kick free from interference or tackle from an opponent. In kicking for goal or kicking to position in field play, a mark gives an obvious advantage. It is equally important as a defensive skill because intercepting the ball by marking can thwart an attacking move. So, an ability to mark safely and surely is an advantage for all players, but particularly for those playing key attacking or defensive roles.

CHEST MARKING

Keeping your eyes on the ball is fundamental to taking possession of it in any way, including the mark. You need to watch the ball into your hands or onto your chest. Lack of confidence, concern at being tackled and a premature look to where you will dispose of the ball are the main reasons for losing eye contact with the ball and making a ball-handling mistake.

The safest form of mark is the chest mark because you can use your body to assist in the catch and to protect the ball from an opponent. In the wet, with the ball slippery and heavy, every attempt should be made to mark the ball on the body (figure 4.1), particularly for young or inexperienced players.

Figure 4.1   Chest Mark

PREPARATION

1. Eyes on the ball
2. Move in line with the ball
3. Arms ready to wrap around and cradle the ball
4. Elbows close together and close to the sides
5. Hands and fingers spread, with palms facing the ball
6. Shoulders hunched
7. Move to meet the ball

Misstep

You misjudge the ball or it is intercepted.

Correction

Approach the ball in a direct line to its flight. Do not wait for the ball to come to you. Move quickly and confidently to the ball.

To execute a chest mark, move confidently in line with the ball to meet it. Your body needs to be directly behind the ball. Do not wait for the ball to come to you because this makes it easier for an opponent to spoil by punching away or intercepting it.

As the ball approaches, your body and arms are prepared to wrap around and cradle it as it hits your chest. Position your arms like a scoop with your elbows bent and close to your sides; spread your fingers and turn your palms towards the ball from beneath. Your shoulders should be hunched as you lean forwards to form a pocket into which the ball will fall. To make the pocket for the ball deeper and surer, lift one knee up close to your elbows. If the ball is slippery or if you are falling or sliding, it is even more important to form the pocket properly.

If the ball to be marked is coming in low, you will need to do a low take (figure 4.2)—that is, bend at both the knees and the hips.

Figure 4.2   Low Take

a b c

PREPARATION

1. Eyes on the ball
2. Move in line with the ball
3. Arms ready to wrap around and cradle the ball
4. Elbows close together and close to the sides
5. Hands and fingers spread, with palms facing the ball
6. Shoulders hunched
7. Fingers pointing to the ground
8. Bend at the knees and hips
9. Move to meet the ball

EXECUTION

1. Body wraps around the ball, hugging it to the chest
2. Elbows close to the sides
3. Knees bent
4. Body flexed at the waist

FOLLOW-THROUGH

1. Roll onto the ground

Misstep

The ball bounces off your chest.

Correction

If you lift or turn your head away from the ball, your arms will try to wrap around the ball at the wrong time. Keep your head down and your arms, chest and head like a letter C into which the ball will come. As you receive the ball, wrap your arms under it and hug it to your chest. Keep your elbows close together.

Misstep

The ball slides through your arms and drops to the ground.

Correction

If you try to bear hug the ball with your elbows spread wide, you will likely lose it. Keep your elbows close together when wrapping your arms about the ball.

As the ball arrives, wrap your arms and body around it, with your forearms clasping it to your chest. Keep your elbows close to your sides. When you are in this hunched position, the ball should be secure even if you fall or get bumped.

Note that senior, well-skilled players sometimes will take the ball in front of their bodies in their hands, particularly when taking a handball. In fact, some coaches demand this because the ball is immediately in the hands for a quick handball, which is so much a part of today's play-on football. It also makes it more difficult for a defender player to spoil the marker (see step 9) by punching the ball away before it can be caught. However, if you are a beginning player, try to take the ball on your chest.

Chest marking is the surest way of taking a mark, and the principles of eyes on the ball and going to meet the ball are fundamental to successfully completing the mark.

Chest-Marking Drill 1. *Throw and Catch*

Using an underarm throw, throw the ball high. Run to position yourself to catch it using a chest mark. Have 10 tries.

To Increase Difficulty

- If you are confident with your kick, instead of throwing the ball, kick it high, run to position under it and catch it using a chest mark. Have 10 tries. Only count it as a try if you are able to get to the ball.

Success Check

- You successfully complete the mark.
- The ball doesn't bounce off your chest or fall to the ground between your arms.

Score Your Success

Chest mark 10 out of 10 = 5 points

Chest mark 5 to 9 out of 10 = 3 points

Your score ___

Chest-Marking Drill 2. *Run and Mark*

A partner either throws or kicks the ball to you. You run to meet the ball (do not wait for it to come to you) and mark it on the chest. If the ball is high, leap to take it. If it is low, bend at the knees and the hips. Remember to wrap your arms around it and keep your elbows close to your sides. Kick the ball back to your partner. Have 10 tries and then change roles with your partner.

To Increase Difficulty

- Have the ball thrown to either side as you approach so that you have to adjust to get behind the ball to take it.
- Have the ball thrown below knee height so that you take the ball, fall and roll.
- Use a rebound net to make the ball come at various heights and angles.

- Have another player apply pressure by attempting to spoil (see step 9) from behind. This will lead on to the hand mark in front of the chest.

Success Check

- You successfully complete the mark.
- The ball doesn't jar loose when you hit the ground on taking a low chest mark.
- Once you have completed the mark, take the ball in your hands and be ready to dispose either by hand or foot.

Score Your Success

Chest mark 10 out of 10 = 5 points

Chest mark 5 to 9 out of 10 = 3 points

Your score ___

Up There Cazaly

The unofficial anthem of Australian football says it all—'Up there Cazaly'. The soaring spectacular mark is what excites devotees to the game and astounds those unfamiliar with it. Captured on still photographs, leaps using other players' backs to catapult themselves to great height to mark the ball have immortalised players such as McKay, Jesaulenko and Pratt.

Television, particularly with its instant replay facility, means that we see more high marking in modern-day football. Fans expectantly watched Warwick Capper and Tony Modra as high balls were kicked in their direction. Ashley Sampi's 2004 'Mark of the Year' defied gravity and belief. Gary Ablett added another dimension in taking the freakish mark, contorting his body every which way, often crashing heavily to the ground cradling the ball in his arms.

However, two marks have recently captured the imagination and awe of all who have seen them. Jonathon Brown of Brisbane and Nick Reiwoldt of St. Kilda not only displayed uncanny athleticism and ball sense, exquisite timing and exceptional ball control but also unbelievable courage in taking their spectacular marks while running with the flight of the ball and jumping into packs of players coming at speed from the opposite direction. Reiwoldt in particular had the crowd holding its breath as he took the mark as he was hit from the front and then cartwheeled over players and crashed into the knees of an incoming defender. 'Up there Cazaly!'

OVERHEAD MARKING

Every footballer wants to take overhead marks. It is a difficult skill and shows a measure of football ability to be able to do it successfully. Figure 4.3 confirms that marking is a complex skill involving judgment, positioning, timing, hand–eye coordination and an ability to leap, grip the ball and land safely, often while one or more other players are contesting you.

Figure 4.3 | Overhead Marking

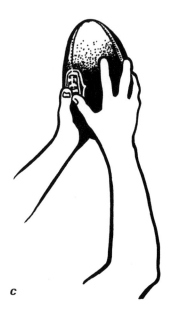

a

TAKEOFF

1. Eyes on the ball
2. Head up
3. One-foot takeoff
4. Arms lifted up and forwards

b

THE TAKE

1. Eyes on the ball
2. Head up
3. Arms parallel
4. Elbows slightly bent
5. Fingers, wrists and arms in a straight line
6. Take the ball in front of the head

c

HANDS

1. Hands slightly cupped
2. Fingers spread but not stiff
3. Thumbs behind the ball

Misstep

You have poor timing and position when trying to mark.

Correction

Make a positive direct approach to the ball with your eyes on it.

Misstep

The ball is easily spoiled by defenders.

Correction

Time your run and your leap so that you are jumping up at the ball rather than running or standing under it. Take the ball out in front of your head at arm's length.

Your eyes need to be on the ball all the time, through the approach, the leap and the take of the ball. Do not drop your head!

Your approach is best made in a direct line with the flight of the oncoming ball, although you may be thwarted by other players. If so, it is even more important to keep eye contact with the ball.

Some marks are made from a two-footed takeoff, but generally the leap for the ball is from one leg with the forward knee providing much of the momentum for the flight. This knee also provides some protection for the front of the body and, occasionally, additional lift by pushing off another player.

Early in the leap, lift your arms upwards and forwards of your body. Your arms should be almost parallel as you reach for the ball; your elbows should remain slightly bent.

Aim to take the ball above and in front of your head, where it is easier to keep your eyes on it. Take the ball at the earliest moment possible, when it is difficult for an opponent to spoil. Your hands should be slightly cupped with your fingers spread and thumbs towards the back of the ball. Your hands should not be stiff but flexible, ready to wrap around the ball as you receive it.

Close your fingers around the ball as you make contact. Your thumbs should be close together to prevent the ball from slipping through your hands. This is especially important when the ball is wet.

Overhead-Marking Drill 1. *Kick and Catch*

Kick the ball straight up and as high as you can. Mark the ball using chest marks for the first 10 and overhead marks for the next 10. Leap to meet the ball each time.

Success Check

- You feel confident in leaping for the ball.
- Use a one-foot takeoff to get height in your leap.
- Relax your hands and fingers so the ball doesn't bounce from them.

Score Your Success

Mark 20 out of 20 = 5 points

Mark 15 to 19 out of 20 = 3 points

Mark 11 to 14 out of 20 = 1 point

Your score ___

Overhead-Marking Drill 2. *End-to-End Marking*

For players of all levels, end-to-end kicking is a basic activity for both chest and overhead marking and for kicking practice. Stand 25 to 30 metres from a partner. Kick the ball so it can be marked. The ball is kicked so that the players have to move to take the ball. Try always to take an overhead mark, but if the ball is kicked poorly, get to where you can take a chest mark. Here positioning and timing are added to the basic practice.

To Increase Difficulty

- Players who have mastered marking should try one-handed marking. First use regular chest marking; then try to take the ball in only one hand.

Success Check

- Time your movements to get into position early to take the ball.
- Watch the ball all the time and keep your head up.

Score Your Success

Each mark is worth 1 point. Subtract 1 point if your kick is so bad that your partner can't mark it. This is a competitive drill; try to earn more points than your partner.

Score more points than your partner = 5 points

Score fewer points than your partner = 0 points

Your score ___

Overhead-Marking Drill 3. *End-to-End Kicking in Pairs*

In this drill one player attempts to mark while his partner makes only a token effort to mark from behind. Players are in pairs about 30 metres apart (farther for those better skilled). Players alternate kicking the ball to the other group. The ball is kicked high to encourage overhead marking. Players alternate positions after each kick so that they have a chance to practise both marking and pressure positions. The rear player does not attempt to spoil at this stage. Have 10 attempts each at marking.

Success Check

- Move into position to take the mark by judging the flight of the ball.
- Take the ball with your arms outstretched to avoid a possible spoil.
- You get experience of marking the ball while feeling an opponent's pressure against you.

Score Your Success

Do not drop one mark = 5 points

Drop one or two marks = 3 points

Drop three or four marks = 1 point

Your score ___

Overhead-Marking Drill 4. *Competitive Marking*

The setup is the same as for the end-to-end-kicking-in-pairs drill, but now both players compete for the mark. This can also be done with the kicker trying to kick the ball slightly to the side of the competing players (figure 4.4), so that the player closer to the ball tries to hold position to prevent the other from positioning to mark the ball. Players alternate positions after each kick.

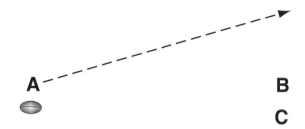

Figure 4.4 Player A kicks the ball slightly to the side of players B and C.

Success Check

- Move into position to take the mark by judging the flight of the ball.
- Take the ball with your arms outstretched to avoid a possible spoil.
- You get experience of marking the ball while feeling an opponent's pressure against you.

Score Your Success

This is a competitive drill; try to earn more points than your partners. Each mark is worth 1 point. Subtract 1 point if your kick is so bad it can't be marked.

Score more points than your partner = 5 points

Score fewer points than your partner = 0 points

Your score ___

HAND MARKING

To reduce the likelihood of the ball being punched away by a defender, attempt to take the ball as early as possible and out in front of your head and body (figure 4.5). This is called hand marking and can be done with relative ease when the ball comes in flatly as you run towards it. The principles of the hand mark are similar to those of the overhead mark except that you do not leap and you take the ball a little more forwards.

Figure 4.5   Hand Marking

1. Eyes on the ball
2. Arms parallel
3. Elbows slightly bent
4. Wrists cocked
5. Thumbs behind the ball
6. Take the ball well in front of the head

Misstep

The ball drops loose from your hands.

Correction

If the ball bounces off your hands, your hands may be too far behind the ball. Keep firm wrists with your thumbs behind the ball and fingers spread to either side. If the ball is wet, slippery or heavy, the hands should come a little more behind the ball.

Whichever marking technique you use, attack the ball with confidence that you will mark it. Judgment and timing are essential in marking. Judgment of the flight of the ball and the positions of the other players are vital, as is the timing of the leap. These are affected by your confidence.

When leading to take the ball on the chest, go to the ball hard. Your opponent will be doing so also, but if you can keep one step ahead, he will not catch you and he will have a hard time spoiling the ball.

Generally adopt the front position when going for a mark. However, this is subject to several factors. The front position is essential if the ball is dropping steeply as with a very high kick or when the ball has been kicked into the wind. If the ball is carrying, as when there is a following wind, the back position may be better. If the ball holds its flight, the player with a run from the back or the side will have the sit (the best position) and be able to leap onto the pack going for the ball.

Once you have taken the mark, be prepared to use the ball to your team's advantage. The job is not completed by taking possession.

Use your voice. If you are in position to mark, call to teammates that you will take it. If a teammate is in a better position, call to him to take the ball. Urge him on strongly and do not compete with him. Remember, only one person can mark the ball. If the ball is within 5 metres, you can block an opponent to help your teammate take possession.

Above all, *keep your eyes on the ball*. Regardless of how high you can leap or how strong your hands are, if you do not keep your head up and eyes on the ball, you will not take a consistently safe overhead mark. Avoid dropping routine marks and take more of the spectacular ones by using basic techniques correctly.

Misstep

You don't watch the ball.

Correction

Fix your eyes on the ball throughout its flight until it is in your hands. Do not duck your head. Take the ball in front of your head so you can watch it into your hands.

For the following drills a rebound net is extremely valuable in providing variability of speed and trajectory. Either a player can underarm throw the ball into the net himself and take the rebound or a partner or coach who is standing behind the rebound net can throw the ball down onto the net. A rebound net attached to a wall about 3 metres above the ground and angled slightly downwards is a valuable tool for players to practise overhead marking as well.

Hand-Marking Drill 1. *Throw and Catch With Hand Marking*

From about 3 metres away underarm throw the ball against a wall at about waist height and catch it in your hands in front of you as it rebounds. Complete 25 rebounds.

To Increase Difficulty

- Start closer to the wall and throw the ball harder at the wall. This will give you less time to judge and take the rebounding ball.

Success Check

- Watch the ball.
- Have your arms outstretched with elbows only slightly bent as you take the ball.
- Fingers and hands should be relaxed.
- Have your shoulders square to the wall when you take the ball.

Score Your Success

23 to 25 rebounds caught = 5 points

20 to 22 rebounds caught = 3 points

17 to 19 rebounds caught = 1 point

Your score ___

Hand-Marking Drill 2. *Run and Hand Mark*

Standing about 10 metres away, a partner either throws or kicks the ball about chest height to you. Run to meet the ball (do not wait for it to come to you) and hand mark it. Take the ball in your hands in front of your body and face. Have 15 tries and then change roles with your partner.

To Increase Difficulty

- Have the ball thrown to either side as you approach so that you have to adjust to get behind the ball to take it.
- Use a rebound net to make the ball come at various heights and angles. Take the ball and handball it to a partner or target on either side.
- Have another player apply pressure by attempting to spoil (see step 9) from behind.

Success Check

- Take the ball while moving forwards.
- Take the ball in both hands and be prepared to handball to either side.
- Don't break stride or jump into the air as you take the ball.

Score Your Success

Clean hand takes 15 times out of 15 attempts = 5 points

Clean hand takes 12 to 14 times out of 15 attempts = 3 points

Clean hand takes 10 or 11 times out of 15 attempts = 1 point

Your score ___

Marking Drill 1. *Reflex Marking*

This drill is intended for more advanced players because it requires some good kicking ability and provides limited time to see, judge and take the ball.

Stand about 5 metres from your partner facing him. Kick the ball from one step so that he has to take it in the hands in front of the chest or face. He then kicks it back to you. Have 20 kicks and marks each. Score 1 point for each caught ball. Subtract a point from your total if your kick is out of the target zone (above the waist but no more than head height).

Success Check

- Take the ball cleanly without fumbling.
- Thumbs should be a little behind the ball to stop it.
- Watch the ball.

Score Your Success

Score 18 points out of 20 = 5 points

Score 15 to 17 points out of 20 = 3 points

Score 12 to 14 points out of 20 = 1 point

Your score ___

Marking Drill 2. *Marking in Packs*

In groups of three or four players about the same height and size and about 25 to 30 metres apart, practise end-to-end kicking and marking. Do this for about 10 minutes. Try approaching the ball from the sides and back of the pack. How many marks can you take? If the ball is not marked, follow it up on the ground, gather it and kick it high to the other pack.

- When attempting to mark in the pack, keep your head up.
- Move to position to leap at the ball.
- If the ball drops short, try to take front position and mark the ball out in front.
- If the ball falls to the ground, swoop on it to practise your gathering skills.

Score Your Success

Make 5 marks = 5 points

Your score ___

Success Check

- Watch the ball in flight and into your hands.

MARKING SUCCESS SUMMARY

Not all players will have the same number of opportunities to take overhead marks in a game; this skill is more the province of larger and key position players. Even then, some marks require strength and courage to stand under the ball. Others will need the ability to spring, athleticism and timing to get high in the air. All players, however, love practising to take the big one.

There's no excuse for dropping a chest mark, particularly if you are not under pressure from an opponent. All players must practise the chest mark because anyone could well be in a position to take one during a game. The nature of the modern game is such that regardless of the type of mark taken, the player needs to be ready to move the ball either by getting back quickly to take his kick or by handballing it. He will have time to reflect on the big mark after the game.

Chest-Marking Drills

   1. Throw and Catch   ___ out of 5

   2. Run and Mark   ___ out of 5

Overhead-Marking Drills

   1. Kick and Catch   ___ out of 5

   2. End-to-End Marking   ___ out of 5

   3. End-to-End Kicking in Pairs   ___ out of 5

   4. Competitive Marking   ___ out of 5

Hand-Marking Drills

   1. Throw and Catch With Hand Marking   ___ out of 5

   2. Run and Hand Mark   ___ out of 5

Marking Drills

   1. Reflex Marking   ___ out of 5

   2. Marking in Packs   ___ out of 5

Total   **___ *out of 50***

In this step if you have scored 40 out of 50, you have demonstrated that you can be an efficient marking player. Identify the drills in which you scored lower and the types of marks you have trouble with. Make sure that you look at why you lost points and set about trying to correct these. In the meantime, move to the next step.

Having taken the mark, the player is in a position to have an uncontested kick to a teammate or to take a shot at goal. A missed kick could lead to a costly turnover or a wasted scoring opportunity. Kicking, inherent in the name of the game 'football', is the next step to success.

Kicking

Australian football employs a variety of kicks. As the game has changed in style, the most common kick has also changed. In today's game of speed and fierce tackling with little room for error, we see great emphasis on placing the ball to advantage. Because of this, the drop punt is the kick most favoured by players and coaches. The flat punt is used as a last resort when a kick needs to be hurried. The torpedo punt is used for distance into the wind, and the reverse punt for kicking from an extreme angle at goal.

Long gone is the place kick, now never seen in games. Much to the disappointment of football purists and traditionalists, the drop kick and stab kick (for both kicks, the ball is kicked on the half volley as it hits the ground) are now rarely employed. With their general riskiness and ineffectiveness in wet weather, these kicks are just not appropriate in today's football, and they will not be discussed in this step. They are, however, still on show at some football training sessions as players experiment with them and in so doing improve their general ball skills.

Because of the speed and pressure of today's football, it is absolutely necessary for players to be able to kick effectively with either foot. Players simply do not have time to get onto their preferred foot. Coaches and opponents know which players have poor disposal skills on one side of the body and defend against them more easily by forcing them onto the wrong foot. The better players are those who kick equally well with either foot, to the point that it is difficult to identify which foot they naturally prefer. These players are able to create and use more options for disposal.

BASIC KICK

Different types of kicks have common elements. We will start with the basic kick.

Hold the ball firmly in both hands with your fingers spread and elbows tucked into the sides to allow the ball to come up naturally in front of the body. Take care to line up the ball, the body, and the target in a straight line.

Run forwards in a straight line towards the target (figure 5.1a). Gauge your approach and speed so that you are balanced and looking to where you will be kicking the ball. Don't stiffen your arms but allow them to move naturally with the run. Your elbows should be still tucked into your sides as you hold the ball above the kicking leg. Don't wave the ball about. Practise in stages by first mastering a one-step approach to the kick, then a walking approach and finally a running approach.

Misstep

The ball goes too high and lacks distance.

Correction

When this occurs, your foot contact on the ball is too high—above knee height. Don't throw the ball into the air but guide it to the kicking foot and lean slightly over the ball. Do not try to correct by shortening the follow-through.

As you are about to execute the kick, move your eyes down to the ball and lean a little over it. When kicking with your right foot, your left hand leaves the ball and is moved to the side to assist in maintaining balance (figure 5.1b). The ball is not dropped from both hands simultaneously. Guide the ball down with your hand from a point in front of your kicking leg in a straight line to your foot; your timing should be linked to the back swing of your kicking leg. Keep the ball in your hand as long as possible. Use both your hand and your eyes to guide the ball to your foot.

Although leg power is important in distance kicking, it is not the only factor involved. Timing and height of contact are also vital, as is a purposeful swing of the leg. The knee and thigh lead the swing, followed by straightening of the lower leg so that your leg is straight as you make contact with the ball or shortly afterwards (figure 5.1c). Swing your leg straight through towards the target, not across the body. Follow through in the same direction to the target (figure 5.1d). Keep your head over the ball. Minimise any body lean backwards.

Strike the ball with your instep (the area covered by the lower part of the laces on the football shoe), keeping the instep firm. In general, the point of contact with the ball should be about knee height, but this will vary. Just remember that the flight of the ball is related to the height of contact. The higher the point of contact, the higher the ball will go. Do not lift your eyes until the kick is completed.

Apart from the reverse punt, the kicking leg follows straight through towards the target and the player continues to run towards the target.

Poor kicking technique causes kicking errors. These errors can relate to any one component or to all four components of the kick—the approach, the preparation and release, the kick and the follow-through.

If you make inconsistent or poor contact with the ball, you may be dropping the ball instead of guiding it to your foot. Relax your arms. Don't wave the ball about during the approach. In the early stages of learning to kick, particularly with a nonpreferred foot, you might find it helpful to hold the ball with the middle finger of your holding hand along the bottom seam of the ball so that you can better place the ball onto your foot. Watch the ball.

Poor positioning of the ball on the foot might also cause the ball to tumble badly or float during flight. The ball will tumble or float if the ball is turned back so that you kick it at the rear with your toes in an upward movement. To counter this, make sure that the back of the ball is pointed to your throat as you hold it and drop it to your foot. Practise holding the ball with one hand under the ball so that it can't be rotated backwards.

An accurate kick is a good kick. If you struggle with poor accuracy when kicking, analyse your technique. Approach in a straight line towards the target. Run straight and kick along the line to the target. It is important to guide the ball from in front of the thigh of your kicking leg straight down to the foot. Make sure your follow-through is straight. Do not kick around corners and, when possible, square your head and shoulders to the target. When kicking for goal, aim at a specific point between and beyond the goal posts—the 7-metre gap is too big and too comfortable a target—and run straight towards the target in the approach.

The distance of the kick depends on a number of factors: timing, a firm foot, head over the ball, contact with the ball at about knee height and a vigorous punch action as the thigh leads the leg action followed by a forceful straightening of the leg.

Figure 5.1 | **Basic Kick**

a

b

APPROACH

1. Correct grip
2. Straight approach to the target
3. Head and shoulders square to the target
4. Natural movement of the arms
5. Arms not held stiffly
6. Ball in front of the kicking thigh
7. Eyes on the target

RELEASE

1. Eyes on the ball
2. Ball guided with one hand
3. Arm straight
4. Arm out to balance
5. Body upright
6. Leg extends back
7. Knee bent

c

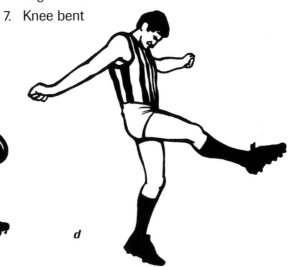

d

EXECUTION

1. Eyes on the ball
2. Leg straight on contact
3. Instep taut, toes pointed
4. Ball contact at instep
5. Contact at knee height
6. Arm out for balance

FOLLOW-THROUGH

1. Arms spread
2. Leg straight
3. Leg towards target
4. Up onto toes

FLAT PUNT

Because of its simplicity, the flat punt is the first kick a player usually attempts. During a game it is effective for covering distance when you are forced to kick hurriedly. However, the ball's trajectory is quite high and it tends to float rather than spin during its flight. Consequently, the ball is adversely affected by wind, is quite difficult to mark and is easily spoiled by defenders.

Hold the ball in front of your kicking leg. Spread your fingers evenly on each side with your hands towards the back of the ball and your thumbs opposite each other just behind the lacing. The middle fingers of each hand should be along the seams on the sides of the ball (figure 5.2).

Point the ball straight ahead and guide it from in-line with your kicking leg straight to your foot. Make contact at and straight down the instep.

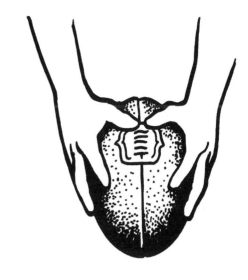

Figure 5.2   Flat-punt grip.

Misstep

You throw the ball into the air or drop it rather than direct it to your foot.

Correction

A practical way to try to overcome this misstep is to practise bouncing the ball onto your kicking foot as it comes off the ground.

Misstep

The ball is not lined up in the direction you intend it to go.

Correction

Don't kick around corners. Straighten your body and kick through the ball. Follow through towards the target, not across your body.

DROP PUNT

The kick used most often in senior football today is the drop punt. It is versatile in that it can be used for accurate goal kicking (in fact, it was first used by forwards shooting for goal), a long field kick, a low punch kick into the wind and a fast, low, accurate pass that is not easily intercepted or spoiled. The drop punt is safe and effective in wet conditions, its flight is predictable and its spin makes it the most suitable for marking.

As with all kicks, the height of contact determines the height of trajectory of the ball. In kicking for distance, your point of contact should be at knee level. For shorter, lower passes, contact the ball just above ground level.

Although there are variations in the way the ball is gripped in preparation for the kick, the most common method is to have it almost vertical, with the top pointing back about 15 degrees so that it points towards your neck (figure 5.3). Grip the ball with your fingers evenly spread and your middle fingers down the side seams on either side of the ball. Your thumbs should be close to the back of the lacing on top of the ball.

To begin the approach to the drop-punt kick (figure 5.4), bend forwards slightly from the hips and waist with your head and shoulders well over the ball in the run-up.

Figure 5.3 Drop-punt grip.

Figure 5.4   Drop-Punt Kick

a

b

APPROACH, FIRST STEP

1. Correct grip
2. Straight approach to the target
3. Head and shoulders square to the target

APPROACH, SECOND STEP

1. Natural movement of the arms
2. Ball in front of the kicking thigh
3. Eyes move to the target

c

d

RELEASE

1. Eyes on the ball
2. Ball guided with one hand
3. Arm straight
4. Arm out to balance
5. Body upright
6. Leg extends back
7. Knee bent

EXECUTION

1. Eyes on the ball
2. Leg straight on contact
3. Instep taut, toes pointed
4. Ball contacts the instep
5. Contact at knee height
6. Arm out for balance

e

FOLLOW-THROUGH

1. Arms spread
2. Leg straight
3. Leg towards target
4. Up on toes

Guide the ball to the foot for as long as possible and kick it at the back of the toes and the lower laces of the instep. The ball should still be almost vertical. Your toes should be pointed. It is the large area of contact between the foot and the ball that gives greater control, making this the preferred kick in almost any condition. It is reliable, predictable and low risk.

The foot kicks through the ball and follows through, imparting a backwards spin to the ball.

Because the kick is used so much for accuracy, it is important to make the run-up and follow-through in a straight line with the target.

If you get poor flight and spin on the drop-punt kick, you probably are turning the ball before striking it with your instep. Try to guide the ball to your foot almost perpendicular to the ground so that contact is on the centre of the bottom point of the ball to impart a backwards spin. Make sure to guide the ball down from in front of the thigh of your kicking leg so that the top seam of the ball is straight down the kicking foot. Do not swing your leg across your body.

TORPEDO PUNT

This kick is also called the spiral punt. When done well, it is very effective. When done poorly, it fails completely in distance, direction and catchability. Because of its high element of risk, the torpedo punt is seen less in today's football. Coaches generally discourage players from using it in general play, and players usually opt to do the much more reliable drop punt. So, as with the drop kick and the stab kick, the torpedo punt may also eventually be consigned to the coaching manuals and pictures and videos of the golden oldies. However, Australian footballers who are very skilled in kicking, and in particular the torpedo punt, are making names for themselves as punters in American football, in which the kick's distance, spin and hang time are vital.

When kicking a torpedo punt, guide the ball to your foot so that it angles across the foot on contact. This imparts a longitudinal spin to the ball that makes this kick effective when the ball is kicked into the wind or needs to gain distance.

The spin also curves the ball's flight, which can be an advantage in some goal attempts, but which makes it difficult to use for passing. As

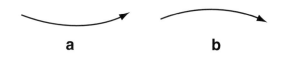

Figure 5.5 Direction of the curve for a torpedo punt: *(a)* right-foot kick; *(b)* left-foot kick.

shown in figure 5.5, the direction of the curve depends on which foot kicks the ball. The torpedo punt is easier to mark than the flat punt, but it is not as preferred as the drop punt.

Figure 5.6 illustrates how to execute the torpedo punt. For a right-foot kick, hold the ball with your fingers spread on each side and slightly on top and with your left hand slightly in front of the lacing and your right hand just behind. This makes the angle of the ball to the target about 10 to 15 degrees.

Guide the ball to your foot with your right hand and contact it at about knee height with the ball at an angle of about 15 degrees to the ground. The ball begins to spiral when contact is made by the lower part of the instep at a slight angle across the foot. Note that the ball is not kicked with the side of the foot.

Figure 5.6   Torpedo Punt

GRIP	EXECUTION	FOLLOW-THROUGH
1. Fingers spread	1. Ball contact across the instep	1. Leg goes straight through towards the target
2. Hands not level		
3. Ball at 10 to 15 degrees		

Because the kick is effective in covering long distances, players often try to kick the ball too hard or impart too much spin by kicking the ball with the outside of the foot. Both of these errors have disastrous consequences.

A poor drop of the ball to the outside of the foot, which leads to slicing the foot across the line of the ball's flight instead of towards the target, will cause the ball to go off the side of the foot. Try to guide the ball to your instep and let the ball's angle give it the required spin. Don't kick down the side of the ball with the side of your foot.

The Torpedo Punt

1976. Princes Park. Malcolm Blight took a mark on the wing side of centre, 70 metres out from goal. The ball was wet and heavy. The final siren sounded with North Melbourne 1 point behind. Knowing the rule that having taken the mark before the siren sounds he was entitled to take his kick at goal, Blight walked backwards 20 metres from the mark and set himself for what most considered an unrealistic and futile attempt. Being so far from goal, most of his teammates and Kangaroos supporters had given the game up for lost and watched more with forlorn hope than expectation. Surrounded by fans who had come onto the ground, Blight ran straight at goal and launched a towering torpedo punt. It was not only accurate but cleared the defending players on the goal line, passing between the goal posts more than 5 metres above ground and giving the Kangaroos an unlikely and memorable 5-point victory. On measurement the kick had traveled over 80 metres.

Years later as a coach, Blight encouraged his players to practise and use the risky torpedo punt with the proviso, 'Have a go, but if the first one doesn't work, give it up for the day and try it again next match'.

REVERSE PUNT

During games, the attacking team tries to position the ball in front of the goals at an angle that allows a relatively easy kick to score. Good defence will prevent the centering of the ball, and a player may be forced to shoot for goal from a tough angle. He can try to improve his chances by using a kick with a curved flight. For instance, a right-footed player may try a torpedo-punt kick from the left side of the goals.

A right-footed player from the right side may attempt to use a reverse punt. To do so he will aim at the imaginary target (T) and use the reverse curve to kick the goal (figure 5.7).

The reverse punt (figure 5.8) has proven successful not only in kicking for goal but also in field play when the player is caught on the wrong foot and needs to get the ball away at an angle to a teammate. This carries a high element of risk, however, and should be used only as a desperate measure. Players are better served by learning to kick with both feet.

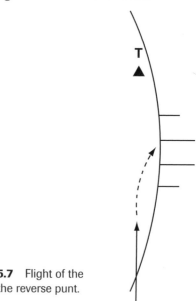

Figure 5.7 Flight of the ball for the reverse punt.

Figure 5.8 | Reverse Punt

PREPARATION
1. Ball at 45 degrees
2. Guiding hand forward

a

58

b

c

EXECUTION	**FOLLOW-THROUGH**

EXECUTION

1. Contact at the back of the ball
2. Foot swinging across the line of flight
3. Ball parallel to the ground

FOLLOW-THROUGH

1. Follow through away from the direction of the ball's flight

---

Hold the ball end to end at about 45 degrees to the line to the target with the guiding hand holding the front of the ball. Hold the ball so that when you release it, it will contact your foot almost parallel to the ground. Run in a straight line towards your imaginary target.

Kick the ball with your instep, using your judgment about the point of contact. The farther from the centre of the ball you make contact, the greater the angle from the line to the imaginary target that the ball will diverge. The greater the distance required, the closer to the middle of the ball you should make contact.

In the follow-through, the leg slices behind the ball on contact and moves slightly away in the direction opposite the ball's flight.

The reverse punt is not easy to execute. The major problem is in gauging the angle required for the curved flight. If the angle is too narrow, the ball will fly past the goals. If the angle is too sharp, the ball will fall short of the goal. Identifying an imaginary target to run and kick towards is a matter of practice. Once you have picked the target, try to ignore the goal posts.

KICKING TIPS

Some kicks used in Australian Rules are unconventional and difficult to plan for or practise. The soccer kick off the ground can be used effectively when the ball and ground are very wet and slippery and when you are under pressure, making it risky to attempt to pick up the ball. This is particularly so when hotly pursued while running into goal even when the ball is dry. Some players become very adept at kicking the ball along the ground, often curving and bouncing around players and goal posts.

A rarely used kick that generally is used only as a last resort close to goal is the kick on the volley. Equally spectacular when it comes off is the kick over the head or shoulder, again usually at goal. More often seen is the tumble kick used to kick the ball away from opponents into space near the boundary line. Most of these are low-percentage kicks that are used as last resorts. However, the skilled player does have them in his bag of tricks and is able to use them on the rare occasions when he cannot use the more conventional kicking styles.

Learning to master kicks is a little like the ball-handling drills seen in step 1. Players will experiment and muck about with kicking the ball by themselves, with a partner or in small groups. Although in most practice sessions players will concentrate on kicking correctly, they should have time to experiment with the ball and what they can do with it. Kids of all ages (including the big kids of the AFL) will use different targets and invent new kicks and scoring systems as they hone their ball-handling and kicking skills. And invariably at some time during matches miracle goals will be scored or a teammate found by those funny kicks practised at the start or end of a training session. Even the drop kick and the stab kick get aired off at times, but not so the place kick—that would be too outrageous!

Who Said It Was Luck?

The traditionalists can be heard criticising players 'mucking about' with 'funny' kicks at training. 'They should be practising their passing and kicking for goal'. Andrew McLeod is one player who tries different things when kicking the ball while waiting for training to begin—kicking with the outside of the foot, making foot contact on different areas of the ball, experimenting with different bounces, spins, flights of the ball and the like.

Football Park, 27 May, 1995. Pouring rain. Adelaide versus Hawthorn. It was the last minute of the game with Adelaide 4 points behind and deep in the forward pocket. McLeod, hard up against the boundary line and surrounded by defensive opponents, gathered the ball. It was heavy and the angle to goal acute. An attempted high kick straight at goal would have had little chance to score a goal even if it cleared the opposition attempts to smother or at least touch it. He chose instead to 'grub' the ball along the ground around players on a curved, seemingly erratic path towards goal. It bounced and skidded 30 metres, eventually going through the goals to give Adelaide an important and unlikely win.

Luck? Yes, some. But imagination, invention and practice gave McLeod the confidence to try something different. Over the years players such as Daicos, Ablett, Modra and indeed McLeod have scored too many goals in similar fashion for it to be just luck. They prepared for it, perhaps by just 'mucking about' with the ball when they had the time to do so.

As you practise your kicking skills, keep these points in mind:

- When possible, straighten your run-up and your body so that your leg swing and follow-through are straight at the target. It helps to get your eyes and shoulders square to the target. Try to avoid kicking around corners.

- When kicking to a moving player, aim at a space in front of the player to allow him to take the ball in front, making it easier for him to play on and more difficult for a defender to spoil.

- To keep the ball low (when passing or when punching the ball into the wind), keep your shoulders and head over the ball and strike the ball at a lower point.

- When kicking for distance, some players have a tendency to rock back so that the kicking leg can straighten earlier, make contact higher and provide greater power. However, the amount of back body lean should be minimised. Greater distance is achieved by better timing with a larger backswing.

- In kicking for goal, particularly from a set shot, narrow the target by picking a spot between and beyond the goal posts at which to aim. It might also help to scratch a mark on the ground near where the ball is marked. When you go back to take the kick, keep the mark directly between you and the goals to guide you in the run-up.

Though almost all drills can involve kicking, some are best specifically for kicking practice. Most of the following drills can be used for all types of kicks except for the reverse punt, which is usually only practised by kicking at goal from near the boundary line.

Kicking Drill 1. *Pair Kicking*

In pairs about 10 to 15 metres apart, kick to your partner (and he to you) while checking for correct technique. Take 20 kicks each.

A very good drill to ensure placement of the ball onto the foot and to develop some power for the kick is to kick over a short distance, say 4 to 5 metres, and not to step at all. Only the kicking leg moves. Have your partner tell you whether the ball was guided to the foot, if it was pointing in the right direction and about the technique of the follow-through.

Success Check

- You consistently get the ball to your partner so he can take it without moving.

- The kick looks good. It spins well (backwards) and doesn't float.

Score Your Success

20 kicks correctly executed and received = 5 points

13 to 15 kicks correctly executed and received = 3 points

10 to 12 kicks correctly executed and received = 1 point

Your score ___

Kicking Drill 2.   *Square Ball*

Increase the space between you and your partner and kick for distance. First kick high and long. Then try low and long kicks. You can make this competitive by playing square ball. Set up two 5-metre squares 30 to 35 metres apart (closer for younger players). From one square, kick to your partner, who is standing in the other square (figure 5.9). Score 3 points if your partner can mark the ball, 2 points if he takes it with one foot in the square and 1 point if it bounces into the square. Take 3 points off your score if you drop one of your partner's kicks that comes into your square. Have 10 kicks each.

Figure 5.9   Setup for square-ball drill.

Success Check

- You consistently have the ball going into the target area.

Score Your Success

Score 26 to 30 points = 5 points

Score 21 to 25 points = 3 points

Score 16 to 20 points = 1 point

Your score ____

Kicking Drill 3.   *Square Ball With Moving Player*

This drill is designed to practise kicking in front of the moving player. The setup is the same as for square ball. Set up two 5-metre squares 30 to 35 metres apart. From one square, kick to the other square. Your partner should be standing 10 metres outside his square when the ball is kicked. He runs into the square to take the mark. Score 3 points if your partner can mark the ball, 2 points if he takes it with one foot in the square and 1 point if it bounces into the square. Take 3 points off your score if you drop one of your partner's kicks that comes into your square. Have 10 kicks each.

Success Check

- Your partner is able to take the ball in the square.
- You take the ball on the full from your partner's kick.

Score Your Success

Score 26 to 30 points = 5 points

Score 21 to 25 points = 3 points

Score 16 to 20 points = 1 point

Your score ____

Kicking Drill 4.   *Competitive Goal Scoring*

Place 10 markers at various distances and angles from the goal (figure 5.10). Each player will have one shot at goal from each of the markers. Player A takes the first kick. Player B stands with hands in the air at the first marker (this is called *standing the mark).* Player A kicks at goal over player B and gets 6 points for a goal or 1 point for a behind.

Player B immediately sprints after the ball, recovers it and kicks it to player A, who has moved to the marker. Player B runs back past player A, who handballs to player B. Player B now takes the kick for goal. Player A recovers the ball and passes it back to player B, who has moved on to the second marker and so on.

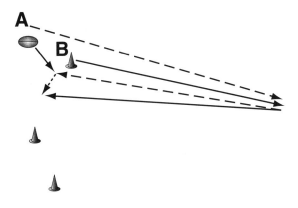

Figure 5.10 Setup for competitive-goal-scoring drill.

Success Check

- Keep your head over the ball as you kick.
- Aim at a specific target between and behind goals at which to kick.
- Follow through with your kicking leg towards the target.

Score Your Success

Score more goals than your partner = 5 points

Score fewer goals than your partner = 0 points

Your score ___

Kicking Drill 5. *Kicking to the Lead*

From both standing and running starts, kick the ball to a leading partner (see step 8). Concentrate on kicking to the front of the movement. Have the leading player come from a variety of angles–towards, from the side, dropping back. Take 20 passes.

Success Check

- Your partner is able to take the ball without breaking stride.
- The ball is never kicked behind the leading player.

Score Your Success

Complete 17 to 20 passes = 5 points

Complete 13 to 16 passes = 3 points

Complete 10 to 12 passes = 1 point

Your score ___

Kicking Drill 6. *Target Ball*

Practise kicking at stationary targets such as the goal and behind posts, the gate, cones and specially built targets. Too often the receiver makes the kick look good because he makes position to receive the ball and is able to adjust his pace, position and distance so that a less-than-perfect kick looks good. A good way to get feedback on your accuracy is to kick to players who are directed not to move. If they can catch the ball without moving from their positions, you know you have kicked accurately.

In groups of four, form up in relay fashion, two at either end 30 metres apart (figure 5.11). The

Figure 5.11 Setup for target-ball drill.

ball is kicked to the receiver. The kicker scores 4 points if the receiver can catch the ball without moving his feet, 3 points if the receiver jumps into the air to take the ball above his head, 2 points if the receiver can take the ball but must take one step (in any direction) to do so, 1 point if the player has to move both feet to take the ball, and 0 points if the player can't catch the ball. After kicking, the kicker runs through and touches the receiver on the shoulder. The receiver then moves off to kick to the other end. Continue until every player has had 10 kicks.

Success Check

• Watch the target as you run up and then watch the ball onto your foot as you kick.

• Don't drop the ball but direct it to your foot by hand.

• Let your leg follow through in a straight line to your target. (If your leg wasn't attached to your body, your partner should be able to catch it.)

Score Your Success

Score 35 to 40 points = 5 points

Score 30 to 34 points = 3 points

Score 25 to 29 points = 1 point

Your score ___

Kicking Drill 7. Pressure Kicking

Three players are needed for this drill. Have some markers near a wall be a goal. Place a kicking marker about 25 metres away (figure 5.12). Player A handballs to player B, who is running fast from the marker and is chased by player C, who tries to put two hands on player B to simulate a tackle. Player B has a running shot at goal and scores a point for every goal. Player B recovers the ball, player A becomes the chaser and player C the kicker. Have 10 tries each at kicking for goal under pressure.

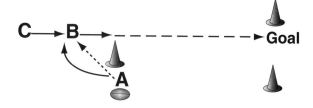

Figure 5.13 Less-difficult variation of pressure-kicking drill. Player A blocks player C, giving player B more time to score.

Success Check

• Watch the ball into your hands, look at the target, then at the ball as you execute the kick.

• Run straight at the target (goal). Don't get into a position that requires you to kick around the corner.

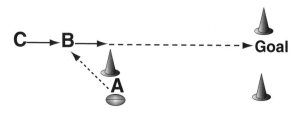

Figure 5.12 Setup for pressure-kicking drill.

To Decrease Difficulty

• Vary the drill so that once player A handballs to player B, he gets into position to block player C (figure 5.13), giving player B a little more time to score the goal.

Score Your Success

Score 10 goals from 10 shots = 5 points

Score 9 goals from 10 shots = 3 points

Score 8 goals from 10 shots = 1 point

Your score ___

Kicking Drill 8. *Chase and Kick*

Play in pairs using markers as a goal. Players stand alongside one of the markers. Player A rolls the ball about 25 metres away (figure 5.14). Player B chases after it, gathers, turns and kicks at goal. Player A gives player B about a 5-metre start and then tries to intercept the shot at goal or to grab hold of player B. Have 10 tries each to see who scores the most goals.

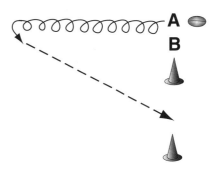

Figure 5.14 Setup for chase-and-kick drill.

Success Check

- Watch the ball and pick it up cleanly.
- Turn your body to face the goals before kicking.
- Be aware of where the pressure is coming from. Baulk and adjust your kick to avoid the pressure.

Score Your Success

Score 10 goals from 10 attempts = 5 points

Score 9 goals from 10 attempts = 3 points

Score 8 goals from 10 attempts = 1 point

Your score ___

Kicking Drill 9. *Receive and Shoot*

Player A runs and kicks the ball between the markers to player B, who takes the ball, turns and handballs to player C, who is running past (figure 5.15). Player C now kicks to player D, who is standing between the markers. Player D handballs to player E (player A's replacement), and play continues. Each player follows the ball to the next group. Continue until every player has had 10 kicks to see who kicked the most goals.

Success Check

- This is a straight-line kick and therefore should be accurate.

- Don't drop the ball when taking it by watching the target too early.
- Run straight towards your target and let the leg follow through straight towards the target.

Score Your Success

Score 10 goals from 10 shots = 5 points

Score 9 goals from 10 shots = 3 points

Score 8 goals from 10 shots = 1 point

Your score ___

Figure 5.15 Setup for receive-and-shoot drill.

Kicking Drill 10. *Letter Kick*

Four players lettered A, B, C and D are in an area about 50 metres square (figure 5.16). All players can move where they like in the square, but they should try to get well away from the others. Player A has the ball and passes it to player B. Player B receives it and passes to player C, who likewise receives and passes to player D, who then passes to player A, and so on. All players are moving all the time. Continue until all players have kicked the ball 10 times. A successful, catchable pass is worth 2 points. Each mark is worth 1 point. Subtract 1 point if you drop a player's pass.

Success Check

- Take control of the ball before looking at your target, but have a feel for where your target is so you can turn towards him once you have the ball.

- Turn your body and kick the ball straight to your partner. Don't kick around corners. It looks fancy and good when it comes off, but it is risky and easily causes turnovers when you miss the target.

- Punch the ball low with your kick to your target.

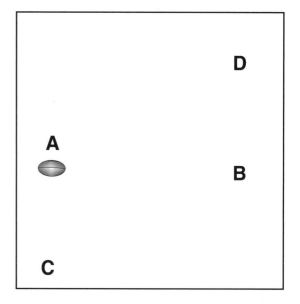

Figure 5.16 Setup for letter-kick drill.

Score Your Success

Score 20 out of 20 points = 5 points

Score 18 or 19 points = 3 points

Score 16 or 17 points = 1 point

Your score ____

Kicking Drill 11. *Space Ball*

This is a fun game in which you can practise both kicking and marking. It is played in pairs or small groups. Set up a no-man's-land of about 5 metres between the teams (figure 5.17). Each team defends a space appropriate to the size of the group.

Kick the ball above head height and across the no-man's-land into your opponent's space. Every time the ball lands in your opponent's space from a kick, your team scores 1 point. Defend your space by catching the ball on the full.

To add variety, incorporate other rules such as the following:

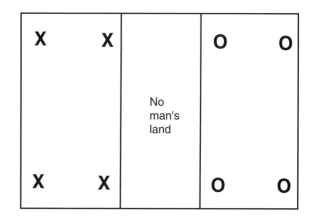

Figure 5.17 Setup for space-ball drill.

- Only marks in the hands are allowed (no chest marks).
- Only drop-punt kicks are allowed.
- Running with the ball is not allowed.
- Handballs are allowed to get the ball closer to the no-man's-land.
- The ball must be disposed of within one second of receiving it.
- Players who catch the ball are not allowed to kick it.
- The ball must be caught with both feet off the ground.

Play for a set time. This is a competitive drill; try to score more points than your opponents.

Success Check

- Don't kick blindly—look for a space as your target. In the game of football you often have to kick to a space.

Score Your Success

Score more than your opponents = 5 points

Score fewer points than your opponents = 0 points

Your score ___

TEAM DRILLS

The number and type of team kicking drills are limited only by the coach's imagination. He will make up and use different drills depending on which aspect of football team play he wishes to demonstrate and have his players practise. The following drills are not meant to be exclusive and are but a few that might be used. With each of the team drills, the size of the area being used and the distance between the groups will depend on the age, size and abilities of the players. Cones, markers, portable posts and other markers can be used to delineate the area.

With each of the following drills, have the groups separated a comfortable distance appropriate for the size and skill of the players. These drills are designed to help players practise accurate kicks and foot passing and therefore should not be compounded by having players try to kick too hard because they are too far apart.

Too many games and training sessions for junior players are conducted on senior-sized ovals. The ground needs to be downsized to suit the age, size and skill of the players. This is most commonly done by using portable goal posts or cones for goals. In the drills that involve goal scoring, this needs to be taken into consideration. Drills should to be adapted to suit the participants or they lose their effectiveness (and the players' interest).

Team Kicking Drill 1. Lane Work

This is the traditional simple team kicking drill. Player A runs towards player B, kicks to him and follows through to the end of the line. Player B kicks to player C, and so on. The drill is made more difficult with a player placed between the end groups so that the players running through have to kick and then follow their kick, receive a handball and then kick accurately while on the run.

Success Check

- Take the ball on the run. This is a leading exercise as well as a kicking one (see step 8).
- Follow your kick so that if you miss the target or the ball is dropped, you will be in place to receive a handball from the player who recovers the ball.

Team Kicking Drill 2.   *Eight-Point Crossover*

Player A kicks the ball to player B, who marks and handballs to player C, who is running past at right angles (figure 5.18). Player C kicks to player D, who marks and handballs to player E, who is on the move and who kicks to player F. Player F handballs to player G, who kicks to player H, who gives to player A, and the drill starts again. Players follow the ball to the next group after disposing of the ball.

Success Check

- Watch the ball into your hands. Don't drop the ball because you are watching the target as you receive the ball.
- Once you have kicked the ball, run through quickly to the end of the next group.
- When handballing, put the ball in front of the running player who can take it comfortably.
- Lead straight towards the kicking player.

Figure 5.18   Setup for eight-point crossover drill.

Team Kicking Drill 3.   *Star Kicking*

Player A kicks to player B, who marks and kicks across the ground to player C (figure 5.19). Player C marks and switches the ball to the opposite pocket to player D. Player D marks, kicks to player E at centre half back, who then kicks to player A in the pocket, and the drill starts again. Players follow their disposal to the next group. The coach can add extra balls at his discretion.

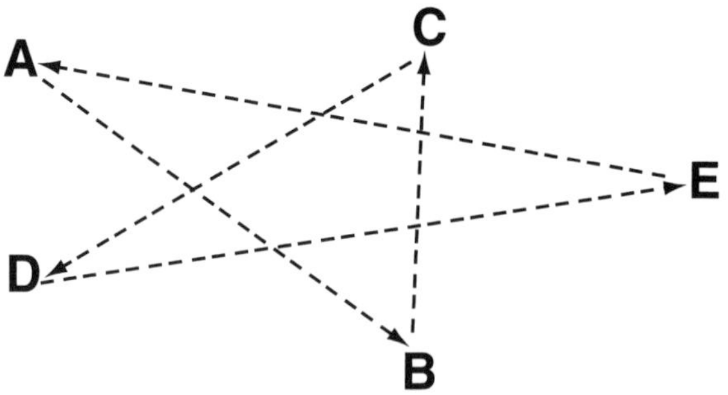

Figure 5.19   Setup for star-kicking drill.

Success Check

- Kick straight to the leading player.
- Be comfortable kicking while travelling at speed towards the leading player.

Team Kicking Drill 4.   *Five-Point Kicking With Goal Scoring*

The ball starts in the goal square with player A (figure 5.20). Player A kicks to player B, who marks the ball and handballs to player C, who is running in the direction of player D. Player C takes the ball and kicks to player D, who is leading directly at him. Player E times his run to receive a handball from player D and kicks at goal while on the run. Players follow the ball to the next group.

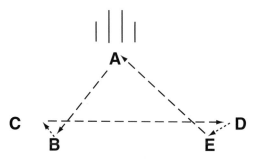

Figure 5.20 Setup for five-point-kicking-with-goal-scoring drill.

Success Check

- Lead straight towards the ball carrier.
- Kick the ball so that the receiver can take it comfortably. Do not make it a contest for him.
- Both the kicker and the receiver should aim to keep the ball in front. It should not get behind the receiver.

KICKING SUCCESS SUMMARY

This step has explained the different kicks used in modern-day football and given numerous examples of how to practise them using challenging drills with scoring. A number have been adapted to be used in group training drills.

Players of all ages and abilities can never practise kicking too much and should look for advice on how to improve their kicks. Technique and timing, and not necessarily raw power and the size of the kicker, will give the distance to the kick. Distance is important; the long goal can lift a side and perhaps win the game. But consistent accuracy in passing the ball to teammates and kicking to position is probably more vital. A misdirected kick can lead to a turnover, destroy a team movement and may set up a scoring opportunity for the opposition. In a senior game there will be around 400 kicks. But not all find their mark because of conditions, pressure from opponents and skill errors. The team that reduces its kicking errors and makes a greater percentage of its kicks effective increases its odds of victory.

Kicking Drills

1.	Pair Kicking	___ out of 5
2.	Square Ball	___ out of 5
3.	Square Ball With Moving Player	___ out of 5
4.	Competitive Goal Scoring	___ out of 5
5.	Kicking to the Lead	___ out of 5
6.	Target Ball	___ out of 5
7.	Pressure Kicking	___ out of 5
8.	Chase and Kick	___ out of 5
9.	Receive and Shoot	___ out of 5
10.	Letter Kick	___ out of 5
11.	Space Ball	___ out of 5
Total		___ *out of 55*

A score of 45 out of 55 shows that you have met the basics of kicking well enough to move on to the next step. However, once again, identify which kicks have caused you to lose points and try to learn why. Continually practise to get them right and improve your accuracy and distance. The next step, running and bouncing, is another skill that is used once you have control of the ball and are moving into attack.

Running and Bouncing

As we have seen, Australian football is an aggressive game that relies heavily on attack. One of the ways that a player can attack and set up offensive patterns is to run with the ball. The rules state that a player may hold the ball for any length of time as long as he is not held by an opponent. If the player runs with the ball, he must bounce it or touch the ground with it at least once every 15 metres from the beginning of his run whether he is running in a straight line or turning or dodging.

Some coaches discourage running with the ball because it tends to delay delivery of the ball downfield. However, if a player can attack the ball at speed, take possession and then accelerate to run his full distance (and with one bounce he is able to run 30 metres), this gives him balance for disposal and adds distance and speed to the attack. Running can be a tactic to get the ball through or over a line when opponents have a defensive edge through size or marking ability. An aggressive runner who will take the ball and challenge opponents to catch him also gains a psychological advantage.

Running aggressively and well is a skill and tactic that should be developed. You must take the ball (either by mark or gather) at speed and then accelerate and balance prior to giving a kick or a handball. Good players recognise and understand the advantages of aggressive running and that the player who does not take the ball at speed and then maintain that speed becomes easy prey for defenders. The skill of baulking while running at speed is also important in off-balancing a defender trying to tackle a running player. The modern characteristics of aggressive, hard-running play demands that players with the ball take on opposition players with aggressive running in the hope that this will draw them in, leaving a teammate in the clear to receive a handball and either continue the run or dispose of the ball by hand or foot in a more controlled and less pressured fashion.

Having run his full distance, the player will need to either dispose of the ball or to bounce it. The run and bounce is an important attacking move that can draw defenders out of position.

Additionally, bouncing the ball is an important skill that players should learn and develop early because of its similarity to the early stages of kicking.

Manassa Magic Becomes Part of Football Folklore

The week after only the second tied Grand Final in AFL/VFL history, in the replay versus North Melbourne, Phil Manassa of Collingwood picked up the ball deep in defence on the members side of the MCG. With no readily available target downfield, Manassa chose to run and run and run. Evading and eluding three North Melbourne opponents, he bounced the ball four times, each time tucking the ball under his arm and running his full 10 metres (as the rule was then) before bouncing again. Coming around the boundary, he got close enough to have a shot at goal. After his fourth bounce, he kicked a memorable goal—all to no avail. Collingwood lost.

RUNNING AND BOUNCING

When running, hold the ball in both hands. From here, firmly guide the ball by one hand down to the ground in such a manner that the ball hits on its bottom front third in front of the foot on the same side of the body as your guiding hand. In this manner the ball will come back to you.

The hand doing the bouncing (and good players are able to use either hand) is more on top of the ball (figure 6.1) than when you are kicking. In fact, the thumb will be past the lace of the ball, and the tip of the fourth finger will be on the side seam. The fingers are spread, and little if any contact is made between the palm of the hand and the ball.

Figure 6.1 The bouncing hand is more to the top of the ball. The fingers, not the palm, control the ball.

Misstep

You are tackled when bouncing the ball.

Correction

Accelerate and run flat out. Do not attempt to bounce the ball when it's not necessary. Do not keep possession when you should kick or handball. Teammates should shepherd or warn the runner of the likelihood of the tackle.

The faster you are moving, the farther in front you will have to bounce the ball so that it comes right back into your hands without slowing your run (figure 6.2).

Figure 6.2 The rebound. The player takes the ball with both hands at waist height.

Misstep

You overrun the ball on the rebound.

Correction

Make sure that you bounce the ball out far enough to allow yourself time to run into it. The ball needs to be bounced with a definite, firm action. Practise to gain confidence.

From the very beginning you should learn to bounce the ball with either hand. This will give you an effective lead to kicking with either foot and allow you to bounce the ball on the side farthest from an opponent.

Many players, novice and experienced, make the mistake of bouncing the ball almost immediately upon possession. This is discouraged because it slows the player down. Also, there is always an element of risk in a bounce. Players should take the ball, accelerate away with it and bounce only after covering 15 metres.

Don't try to bounce when the ground is wet, slippery or muddy. Instead, simply touch the ball onto the ground every 15 metres. Do this by bending at the knees and hips, holding the ball in both hands and touching it to the ground slightly to one side of your body (figure 6.3).

Figure 6.3   Touching the Ball on the Ground

1. Ball held in both hands
2. Knees bent
3. Hips flexed
4. Head over the ball
5. Touch the ground alongside the lead foot

Bouncing Drill 1. *Bouncing*

Regularly practise bouncing the ball. This is not a skill you will use often in games, but it is an essential lead-up to kicking and is invaluable to ball handling. The ball is bounced on the forward bottom quarter (figure 6.4a) and should be directed forcefully to the ground by one hand (figure 6.4b). A proficient player should be able to bounce the ball with either hand.

Figure 6.4a   Bouncing: The ball bounces on the forward bottom quarter.

Figure 6.4b Bouncing: Forcefully direct the ball to the ground with one hand.

Try to master all of the following techniques and remember to switch hands:

- Bounce with one hand and catch with both.
- Bounce with one hand and catch with one.
- Bounce the ball as low to the ground as you can. Now bounce it as close to the ground and as fast as you can.
- Bounce the ball and let it do one complete revolution (backspin) before you catch it. Is the seam pointing directly away from you?
- Even top players find bouncing two balls alternately (one with each hand) a challenge to their ball-handling expertise. Try it and work towards mastering it.

Success Check

- Bounce the ball on the ground. Don't push it towards the ground. (This is achieved more with a 'chopping' action of the arm and straightening the elbow.)
- You are comfortable handling the bouncing ball.
- You have complete control of the ball. It comes back to you and doesn't get away.
- You are able to use either hand to bounce the ball.

Score Your Success

These are stationary drills.

Five bounces with your left hand = 1 point for each bounce you catch

Five bounces with your right hand = 1 point for each bounce you catch

Five bounces with your left hand, ball does one complete revolution (backspin) before you catch it = 1 point for each successful bounce and catch

Five bounces with your right hand, ball does one complete revolution (backspin) before you catch it = 1 point for each successful bounce and catch

Your score _____

Bouncing Drill 2. *Stationary Bounce*

Bounce the ball while standing still. Practise with both hands separately. If you are practising with a partner, have two or three bounces before handballing the ball to him. Copy your partner. If he does a figure eight around the knees or some other ball-handling trick before he bounces, you do the same. If you and a partner both have a ball, see if you can bounce at the same speed. Are you able to use your partner as a mirror while bouncing? Face him and bounce at the same speed; if he is bouncing with his right hand, you will need to bounce with your left.

Success Check

- Bounce the ball on the ground. Don't push it towards the ground. (This is achieved more with a 'chopping' action of the arm and straightening the elbow.)
- Make sure you are able to do the same action with your nonpreferred hand.

Score Your Success

Execute 25 controlled bounces in a row = 5 points

Execute 24 controlled bounces in a row = 3 points

Execute 23 controlled bounces in a row = 1 point

Your score ___

Bouncing Drill 3. *Follow-the-Leader Bounce*

With a partner, play 'follow the leader'. Run at various speeds and bounce the ball every 15 metres. Once you have bounced and caught the ball, handball it into the air or put it on the ground so that your partner, following behind you, takes possession, runs 15 metres, bounces the ball and hands over possession in a similar fashion. Try using specific patterns; for example, zigzag, circle or figure eight while bouncing with the appropriate hand.

Success Check

- Bounce the ball on the ground. Don't push it towards the ground. (This is achieved more with a 'chopping' action of the arm and straightening the elbow.)
- Make sure you are able to do the same action with your nonpreferred hand.

Score Your Success

Complete five successful transfers with your partner after controlled bouncing = 5 points

Your score ___

Bouncing Drill 4. *Run the Maze*

With a partner, scatter 10 markers at some distance from each other (figure 6.5). Your partner then stands between two additional markers about 30 metres from the 10th marker. Run hard at the ball on the ground, pick it up and run the maze pattern, bouncing the ball as you pass each marker. Score 1 point for each successful bounce. As you pass the last one, kick the ball to your partner, who then runs.

Success Check

- Develop a rhythm so that you do not change pace or stride as you bounce the ball.
- Bounce the ball far enough in front of you so you do not break stride as it rebounds into your hands.
- Take the rebounding ball in both hands.
- Have control of the ball at all times as you run with it.

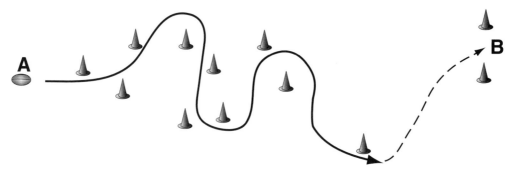

Figure 6.5 Setup for run-the-maze drill.

BAULKING, FEINTING AND TURNING

Part of the aggressive running game is baulking and turning. When you are carrying the ball and are approached by an opponent, do not panic into a hasty disposal. Practise dodging an opponent and placing him out of position for the ensuing play.

Although they can and should be introduced to young players, these skills are regarded as quite advanced. They also incorporate an element of risk. The rules of the game state that if tackled after having had prior opportunity to dispose of the ball, the player is deemed to be holding the ball and has a free kick awarded against him. Do not devote a lot of time to these skills early, however, because mastery may be difficult.

Blind Turn

In the blind turn (figure 6.6), the player is pursued from behind. The player feints (usually by moving the ball to one side), then uses a strong foot action to push off in the opposite direction. If the feint is successful, the pursuer follows the first movement and takes himself out of position.

Figure 6.6 Blind Turn

a

FEINT

1. Feint with the ball
2. Lean towards the ball
3. Head faces the ball

b

PUSH-OFF

1. Strong push-off with the inside leg

(continued)

(continued)

c

FOLLOW-THROUGH

1. Bring the ball close to your body as you turn

2. Balance and accelerate away

Double-Back

An extension to the blind turn is the double-back (figure 6.7). The ball has not yet been gathered. The leading player baulks in one direction and at the same time knocks the ball back with his hand. He then pivots on his track and gathers the ball while running away from his pursuer.

| Figure 6.7 | Double-Back |

1. Bend the knees
2. Flex at the hips
3. Knock the ball back behind
4. Turn back to recover the ball

Baulk

Met from the front, the attacking player has several options. The first is to draw the defender towards him and then handball over the defender's head to a teammate in the clear. But if the attacking player wants to maintain possession, he can try to baulk (figure 6.8). During a baulk, the ball is thrust to one side to give an indication of moving to that side. Then the player pushes off strongly to the other side and swerves past the unbalanced opponent. The baulk is sometimes effectively used for getting past a player standing the mark, allowing the player with the ball to play on.

The attacking player's second option is to baulk and pivot. Here, as the player swerves, he pivots away from the opponent.

Figure 6.8	**Baulk**

a

PREPARATION

1. Feint with the ball to one side
2. Keep the feet apart
3. Lean in the direction of the ball
4. Watch the opponent

EXECUTION

1. Strong push-off with the leg on the ball side

b

c

FOLLOW-THROUGH

1. Bring the ball close to the body
2. Be ready to accelerate quickly

Push and Run

When approaching an unbalanced opponent, you may avoid the tackle by pushing the player in the chest with your open hand and break-ing away in a slightly different direction (figure 6.9). Called a push and run, this is a dangerous movement because the alert defender can apply a tackle. Generally a pass-off is the preferred option.

Figure 6.9 **Push and Run**

PREPARATION
1. Ball held away from the opponent

EXECUTION
1. Ball held away from the opponent
2. Hand flat on the opponent's chest
3. Elbow slightly bent
4. Strong straightening of the arm
5. Push off with the foot closest to the opponent

FOLLOW-THROUGH
1. Accelerate away from the opponent

Holding the Ball

It is important to understand the rule regarding holding the ball. The rule states that a player in possession of the ball and held by an opponent must attempt to dispose of the ball immediately by kicking or handballing. If he had a prior opportunity to dispose of the ball, he will be penalised the moment he is tackled.

The spirit of the rule is to allow a player time to dispose of the ball. However, if he is tackled while baulking, feinting or the like, he will have had that time and will need to dispose of the ball as he is tackled or else be penalised. Therefore, trying to evade a tackle becomes a risk, particularly if a player habitually tries to avoid or break a tackle rather than dispose of the ball.

A player should not be caught if he is running in the open. Safety first dictates that the ball be disposed of by a handball or kick before a tackle is likely. When pivoting, make the turn away from the tackling player and not into him. If a tackle is likely, lift your arms so that they will not be caught and to allow for a handball.

Dodging-and-Turning Drill 1. *Target Dodge*

By yourself, run towards a point post. As you get to the post, baulk or pivot and, having cleared it, handball the ball at the goal post. Try this coming from different angles. Have 10 tries and score 1 point for every hit on the target post.

Success Check

• Maintain your balance and control of the ball as, and after, you dodge and turn.

Score Your Success

Score 10 hits from 10 tries = 5 points

Score 8 or 9 hits from 10 tries = 3 points

Score 6 or 7 hits from 10 tries = 1 point

Your score ___

Dodging-and-Turning Drill 2. *Partner Dodge*

Holding a ball, face your partner. Run towards him, trying to avoid his tackle by using a baulk, twist or spin, and try to hit the target with a handball (figure 6.10). Score 2 points for hitting the target, 1 for missing and none if you are tackled so that you can't handball. Change over and have 10 tries each.

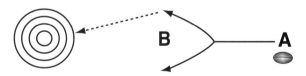

Figure 6.10 Setup for partner-dodge drill.

Success Check

• Keep the ball away from the tackle.

• Remain balanced.

• Be prepared to handball at the target if you are tackled.

Score Your Success

Score 18 to 20 points = 5 points

Score 15 to 17 points = 3 points

Score 12 to 14 points = 1 point

Your score ___

Dodging-and-Turning Drill 3. *Chase and Dodge*

Practise in pairs. One player holds a ball and starts 1 metre in advance of the other. On a signal the two players sprint to a marker 10 metres away, circle it, and run back, with the back player trying to catch and tackle the ball carrier (figure 6.11). The carrier attempts to hit the target with

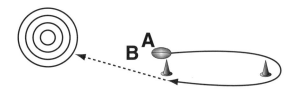

Figure 6.11 Setup for chase-and-dodge drill.

a handball. Score 2 points for hitting the target, 1 for missing and none if you are tackled so that you can't handball. Change over and have 10 tries each.

Success Check

- Be aggressive—you know where you are going, and your opponent has to react to your move. That gives you an advantage.
- Be prepared to handball at the target if you are tackled.

Score Your Success

Score 18 to 20 points = 5 points

Score 15 to 17 points = 3 points

Score 12 to 14 points = 1 point

Your score ___

Dodging-and-Turning Drill 4. *Aggressive Running*

Work with two others, one acting as a starter. Put a ball on the ground 15 metres away. The two contesting stand shoulder to shoulder. On the signal they sprint to the ball to pick it up. A point is awarded to the person getting the ball. A tip: When the signal is given, spread both arms and try to push off your opponent. This exercise can be done around markers, and players try to hold their positions as they round each marker. Have five tries each.

Success Check

- React quickly to your opponent's move-ment.

- Push off your opponent as you start your run.
- Once you have gained the front position, make yourself as difficult as possible to get past.

Score Your Success

Get the ball first on five of five attempts = 5 points

Get the ball first on four of five attempts = 3 points

Get the ball first on three of five attempts = 1 point

Your score ___

Dodging-and-Turning Drill 5. *Sidestep Relay*

This is a relay race for teams of four players. Set up restraining cones or markers 10 metres on either side of the maze. Two players are at each marker. On the signal the first player (who has the ball) carries the ball and sidesteps through the markers as shown in figure 6.12. Once through the maze,

the player bounces the ball once and carries it to the next runner. Keep going until each player has been through the maze, competing against other teams of four.

Success Check

- Players sidestep through the maze.
- Runners' shoulders and hips are kept front on to the running direction at all times.
- Balance and ball control are maintained as the player emerges from the maze and bounces the ball.

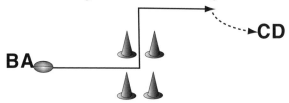

Figure 6.12 Setup for sidestep-relay drill.

RUNNING AND BOUNCING SUCCESS SUMMARY

Manassa's run illustrated how aggressive running can advance the ball while also adding confusion to and placing doubt in the minds of the defenders. Do they come forwards and attempt to tackle and stop the run? If they do, the ball carrier is likely to handball over the defenders to a teammate in the clear. If the defender holds back and plays off the runner, the ball is still being carried forwards into attack.

The important thing for the runner to remember is not to hold on to the ball in a way that gives defenders down the ground time and opportunity to cover their men and fill in space. It is something of a balancing act. The modern coach will encourage his players to run aggressively at their opponents, to challenge them and take them on. This type of confrontation is one of the exciting aspects of the free-flowing game. However, it does carry with it elements of risk. Players need to be confident in their bouncing skills and their ability to use them at top speed.

Bouncing Drills

1. Bouncing   ___ out of 20

2. Stationary Bounce   ___ out of 5

3. Follow-the-Leader Bounce   ___ out of 5

4. Run the Maze   ___ out of 5

Dodging-and-Turning Drills

1. Target Dodge   ___ out of 5

2. Partner Dodge   ___ out of 5

3. Chase and Dodge   ___ out of 5

4. Aggressive Running   ___ out of 5

Total   ___ **out of 55**

If you scored at least 45 points out of 55, you have shown that you are ready to move on to the next step, tackling. If you didn't score at least 45 points, you will need to do some more work in this area or you are likely to be tackled more than you would prefer. That may lead to costly holding-the-ball decisions or losing control of the ball.

Tackling

It is custom in the media compilation of game statistics to record the *offensive* details—the kicks, marks, handballs and goals scored—and not the *defensive* tackles, blocks off the foot, shepherds, spoils or chases. Major awards are made to the top goal kicker and for the mark of the year. Headlines and photographs illustrate the match-winning mark and the impossible goal, but neglect to give equal billing to the desperate smother, the bone-crunching tackle, the effective shepherd or the defensive spoil that may have had as much or even more bearing on the game's result. But the players and coaches recognise the importance of defence. It is not coincidental that many Best Team Man awards go to the players with exceptional defensive skills. In fact, most AFL teams are now appointing defensive coaches.

Defensive skills are characterized by commitment, desperation and discipline. So much good defensive work can be attributed to a player's intense desire to stop his opponents from getting the ball, or if they have it, to stop them from making effective use of it. The valued team player may never win any awards from the media, but he is relied upon to tackle, block, shepherd, spoil, chase and do anything in his power to legally deny the opposition possession. A team of 22 such players would be an awesome opponent.

This step is the first to address a defensive topic—tackling. If a player has possession of the football, he may be tackled. A player in possession of the ball may be tackled and grasped in the area below the top of the shoulders and on or above the knees. The tackle may be from the front, side or behind provided that the tackle from behind does not thrust forwards the player with the ball.

Defenders tackle to stop or at least slow the ball carrier's progress. They hope also to make it difficult for the carrier to dispose of the ball, leading to a free kick for holding the ball. A vigorous tackle may also cause a poor or illegal disposal. This too could lead to a free kick, and it certainly provides a chance for the defensive team to take possession.

A tackle, or even just the threat of a tackle, can create a lot of pressure for the player with the ball. Consider the story of Byron Pickett. In round 18, 2003, with Port Adelaide 2 points down and with less than 90 seconds to play, Hawthorn half back Joel Smith was stuck in no-man's-land on the Great Southern Grandstand wing of the MCG. Byron Pickett was 30 metres away and kept running at him. 'Joel had two options—to kick it or handpass it', Pickett recalled. 'I had to get to him and the ball finished in my lap [as Smith handpassed]'. Pickett handpassed to Lade and kept running to take Lade's

A Scott Salisbury Triple Play

When trying out for Glenelg in the South Australian National Football League, Scott Salisbury was told to go away and play for a district amateur team as he wasn't skilled or quick enough to make it at the senior level. He chose to ignore that advice, persisted and eventually was given a chance. Known for his crunching tackles and 'take no prisoners' approach, Salisbury played in the back pocket in the last line of defence.

Glenelg was playing West Adelaide when an opponent, heading towards goal, took Salisbury on. As he baulked to get past him, Salisbury, eyes riveted to the ball carrier's hips, drove his shoulder into his body and, locking his arms, took both the player and the ball over the boundary line. At the subsequent throw-in, a West Adelaide player gathered the ball and attempted a quick kick at goal. The ever-alert Salisbury launched himself over the player's boot effectively smothering the ball. Another West Adelaide player soccered the loose ball off the ground in the direction of the goal. As it bounced along the ground, Salisbury got to his feet and chased after the ball, diving at it and touching it just prior to it crossing the goal line, saving a major score.

Once deemed unfashionable and not good enough, the tough, uncompromising and totally committed Salisbury went on to play over 200 games for Glenelg and throughout his career was first-choice back pocket for South Australia for State of Origin games. A coach's dream team player, but a nightmare for opponents.

return handpass and kick at goal, completing a 100-metre play with a goal that saved Port from an embarrassing defeat.

In the Pickett story the pressure of a pending tackle in the dying seconds of a game changed the probable result of that game. But all tackles, smothers, spoils and other defensive actions have the potential to do this regardless of when in the game they occur.

Tackling is an aggressive skill requiring a determined commitment backed by strong action. Those who halfheartedly tackle are rarely successful, sometimes get hurt and are usually brushed aside by the opposition.

EXECUTING THE TACKLE

In tackling, watch the player's hips and not the ball (figure 7.1). A good, agile attacker can use ball movement to deceive a tackler into moving in the wrong direction and missing the tackle.

Figure 7.1   Tackling

a

PREPARATION

1. Eyes on the opponent's hips
2. Arms spread
3. Slightly crouched

(continued)

(continued)

b

EXECUTION, FRONT ANGLE

1. Head in close and held up
2. Shoulders and body hard against the opponent
3. Feet on the ground

c

EXECUTION, BACK ANGLE

1. Feet apart
2. Arms wrapped around the opponent
3. Arms pinned to the side

Misstep

The player with the ball is able to break free from the tackle.

Correction

Once you have decided to tackle, move strongly and decisively. A tackle made from a distance with only the arms is easily broken. To prevent this, get in close to your opponent, trying to get your head and shoulders close to his body. Keep your head up.

Strive to be as close to the attacker as possible for the tackle. Keep your head and shoulders tucked in against his body. Keep your head up. Do not jump into the tackle. Keep both feet on the ground.

A player who knows he is about to be tackled will try to avoid having his arms pinned by the tackle. As the tackler approaches, he will lift the ball with both hands high above his head and try to handball quickly off to a teammate (figure 7.2). Therefore, try to include at least one of the ball carrier's arms (or both, preferably) in the tackle to minimise the chance for effective disposal.

Figure 7.2
Freeing the arms.

Misstep

The tackled player is able to dispose of the ball.

Correction

Try to pin one or both arms in the tackle and pull or swing the player off balance.

Try to push, pull or swing the player away from the ball. A player who is on the ground is an ineffective player. However, remember that the rules penalise pushing in the back and slinging once possession has been lost.

Greater balance is gained from starting the tackle from a slightly crouched position and driving upwards. This upwards movement is likely to take the opponent off his feet.

A smaller player can still be an effective tackler of larger players by wrapping his arms about his opponent's body and dropping down to the ground using both players' weight to bring the ball carrier down.

To avoid giving away free kicks to your opponents, remember that the ball carrier can be tackled above the knees and below the shoulders only when he is in possession of the ball. If the ball is dislodged or legally disposed of, you must

discontinue the tackle. If you are tackling from behind, you must not push the carrier forwards as this leads to a free kick for an in-the-back penalty. Drop down when making the tackle so that the movement of both players will be down rather than forwards.

If the player you are trying to tackle is able to get away, check to see if you are watching the ball rather than the ball carrier's hips. Whereas ball movement can easily deceive, the hips signal a dodge early. By running directly at the ball carrier, you commit yourself to the tackle and the carrier has an easier time avoiding you. Watch the hips and stop in front of the ball carrier. He then must commit to a dodge, and in doing so he may become indecisive. By propping, you are better placed to adjust your move to the attacker's. Once you decide to tackle, do so with a strong effort.

Tackling Drill 1. *Partner Tackle*

Face your partner, who stands about 4 metres away. As he runs straight towards you, tackle him (figure 7.3). He gets 2 points if he gets past you or 1 point if he doesn't get past but is able to handball towards a target. He doesn't receive any points if you catch one or both of his arms in your tackle. Do five tackles and then change over.

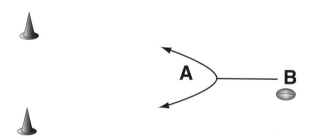

Figure 7.3 Setup for partner-tackle drill.

Success Check

- Watch the player's hips and not the ball.
- Don't commit too early, giving the ball carrier time to evade your tackle.
- Pin his arms to stop him from handballing the ball away.

Score Your Success

Keep your partner to 0 or 1 point out of 10 possible = 5 points

Keep your partner to 2 or 3 points out of 10 possible = 1 point

Your score ___

Tackling Drill 2. *Chase and Tackle*

Play in pairs. Your partner holds a ball and stands 1 metre in front of you, facing away from a target. On a signal both you and your partner sprint to a marker 10 metres away, run around it, and then run back with you trying to catch and tackle your partner as he tries to hit the target with a handball (figure 7.4). Do five tackles and change over.

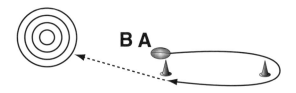

Figure 7.4 Setup for chase-and-tackle drill.

Success Check

- As you catch the ball carrier, pin his arms.
- Drop down to the ground. Don't let your momentum push the ball carrier forwards, giving him a free kick for a push in the back.

Score Your Success

Make more tackles than your partner = 5 points

Your score ___

Tackling Drill 3. *Reaction Tackle*

Play in threes. Players A and B stand facing each other 5 metres apart. Player C rolls or handballs the ball between the players slightly closer to one than the other (figure 7.5). The player closest to the ball picks it up and tries to handball it back to player C. The other player tries to prevent this by tackling and pinning the ball carrier's arms. Score 1 point for each successful tackle and pin. Change over after five tackles, with player C taking the place of either player A or player B.

Success Check

- As you tackle the player, do you have your head placed against his body?
- Keep your head up in the tackle.
- Drop to your knees as you tackle your partner.

Score Your Success

Score more points than both your partners = 5 points

Score more points than one of your partners = 1 point

Your score ___

B

A

Figure 7.5 Setup for reaction-tackle drill.

Team Tackling Drill 1. *One-on-One Competition*

The coach stands out in front of the group, who are in pairs. He kicks, throws or rolls the ball towards the first pair, who battle to pick up the ball and then get it back to him by handballing. The player who does not get the ball tries to tackle the ball carrier and prevent him from returning the ball to the coach. Football rules apply in getting the ball back to him. The coach can vary the drill by having the two players fight for the ball several times in succession.

Success Check

- Your opponent is not able to avoid your tackle.
- You are able to pin his arms to stop him getting the ball back to the coach.
- You do not give away a free kick for an incorrect tackle.

Team Tackling Drill 2. *One-on-Two Competition*

In a fairly restricted area the coach kicks the ball high to player A and player B, who work as a team to run the ball back and handball to the coach (figure 7.6). Player C tries to intercept the ball or to tackle the ball carrier. Only forward ball movement is allowed.

To Increase Difficulty

- Instead of one on two, change it to two on three.

Success Check

- Do not commit too early to allow one player to avoid your tackle and his partner to make space to receive the handball.
- You cause the turnover with a strong tackle.
- You knock the ball loose by your tackle.

Figure 7.6 Setup for one-on-two competition drill.

Score Your Success

Rotate after each effort. Each player has five turns at being the tackler. Earn 1 point if you cause the ball to hit the ground through a tackle.

Three successful tackles = 5 points

Two successful tackles = 3 points

One successful tackle = 1 point

Your score ___

Team Tackling Drill 3. *Tackle Handball Football*

This drill requires teams of four or five players in a fairly restricted area. Goals are 1 to 2 metres wide. No goal keeper is used.

Teams set up on opposing sides facing the goals they are attacking. The coach throws in the ball from the side (figure 7.7). Players battle for possession and attack the opponent's goal. The aim is to get the ball through the goals by handballing. Only handballs will score; no kicking is allowed. No marks are allowed, but free pos-

sessions can be paid. Whenever a goal is scored or the ball goes out of bounds, the opposing team brings the ball into play. Players with the ball can be tackled. This is a very competitive game and quite strenuous if played well, so rotate teams on and off every two to three minutes. As players become more proficient, the game is made more difficult by paying a free possession whenever the ball is dropped or mishandled.

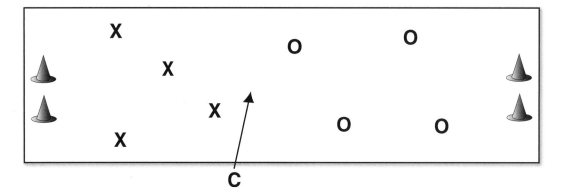

Figure 7.7 Setup for tackle-handball-football drill.

Success Check

- You are able to guard players to prevent a handball option.

- You tackle the ball carrier effectively.
- You do not give any free kicks away for incorrect tackles.

TACKLING SUCCESS SUMMARY

The most spectacular skills and incidents seem to be restricted to the offensive side of the game. No car has ever been presented for the tackle of the year, and certainly (to our knowledge) a list of the best 10 spoils ever has never been published. However, there is nothing more exhilarating than a chase down from behind and eventual tackle bringing a fleet-footed ball carrier to the ground and the crowd to its feet screaming a collective 'BALL!!!'

Such was the case on the 29th of May 2004. One of the AFL's most decorated and quickest players, Shane Crawford of Hawthorn, was running the ball through the centre of the MCG. Confident in his speed, Crawford was not aware of Adelaide Crows young gun Marty Mattner chasing and gaining on him. Mattner brought him down with a perfect tackle from behind and was awarded a free kick. A newspaper article on Mattner praised his ability to run down opponents at full throttle and wrap them up with octopus-like arms, inspiring his teammates. One of those teammates explained, 'When you are watching him chase a player who thinks he is free, get to him and drag him down, there's a turnover and, bang, we are in attack and it results in a shot at goal . . . . He's really inspirational when he does those sorts of things'.

Mattner explained, 'I pride myself on my tackling. When I was younger, tackling was mentioned to me as being a really important part of the game. I took that on board and with it am able to help the team out and put pressure on the opposition'.

Tackling Drills

   1. Partner Tackle   ___ out of 5

   2. Chase and Tackle   ___ out of 5

   3. Reaction Tackle   ___ out of 5

Team Tackling Drills

   2. One-on-Two Competition   ___ out of 5

Total   ___ ***out of 20***

Because the drills in this step have been basically one on one with a 50–50 chance of success, if you have scored 10 out of 20, you have held your own. If you scored less, you might need to spend time with your coach and a tackle bag.

If you scored 20 out of 20, you will contribute well to your team's defensive performance. Now move on to the next step, in which you will be involved in marking contests, as an attacking but also a defensive player.

Leading, Guarding and Standing the Mark

One of the factors that is vital for team strategy is the concept of space. Players will attempt to make space so that they and their teammates can use space. Conversely, defenders will try to close up spaces.

When leading, the player is trying to place himself in the best position to receive the ball from his teammates. Generally he is trying to run quickly away from his opponent into a space where he will have less opposition in marking or gathering the ball. Teammates therefore try to deliver the ball out in front of the leading player so that he can mark it on his chest or out in front of his body, making it difficult for his opponent to intercept or spoil the ball.

Even well-defended opponents will mark the ball during the game. When an opponent marks the ball or when a free kick is awarded, the defender's goal is to prevent the opponent from playing on, giving his teammates time to cover their opponents down the field. This is know as standing the mark, and it is a vital defensive skill.

LEADING

When executing the lead, do not lead too early. You should not lead before your teammate has possession and control of the ball and is in a position to kick it (figure 8.1a). If he has taken a mark or received a free kick, wait until he is back off the mark and is ready to kick. Do not lead while he is going backwards as he will not be able to kick while doing this. The lead will be wasted and the space filled. Lead into your teammate's vision so that he can see you and is not forced off balance in his attempt to dispose of the ball effectively (figure 8.1b).

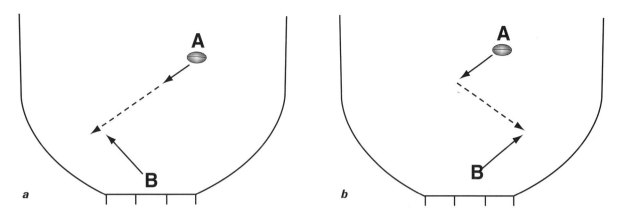

Figure 8.1 Timing and direction of the lead: *(a)* a proper lead in which player A is in control of the ball and is ready to kick it; *(b)* an improper lead in which the leading player (player B) leads to a poor position.

Misstep

You lead too early.

Correction

Wait until the player is in position to kick before you lead. Establish eye contact with him and run hard to a position in front of him to receive the ball. The kicking player should not have to change direction dramatically or kick across his body to kick to your lead.

The lead (figure 8.2) can be in any direction—forwards, to the side or backwards—and can be after a baulk to off-balance the defender. Sometimes the player about to lead will signal the passer as to the direction in which he will be leading.

Figure 8.2	**Leading**

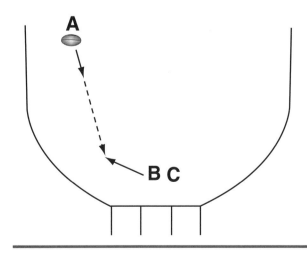

1. Positioning between the defender (C) and the ball
2. Push off from the defender
3. Lead into space

Misstep

As the leading player, you are too easily covered by the defending player.

Correction

Push off from your opponent and run strongly. A halfhearted lead is easily covered and the ball easily intercepted.

The lead should be at full pace. Anything less is too easily covered by the defender. A more experienced player may be able to legally push off from the defender, giving him a metre's advantage that is almost impossible to make up. Positioning early is important here so that as the ball approaches, the defender is not between the ball and the leading player. Conversely, the defending player will try to position himself here and force the leading player to lead to a less advantageous space.

Forward players shouldn't lead deep into the pockets of the ground nor to the defensive side of the ground (see step 12). It is good practice for a forward player who leads for the ball to keep leading even if the ball is not passed to him. Doing so creates space behind for another player to lead into and the ball to be kicked.

Once the ball has gone beyond the leading player, he should turn and go with the ball to be in a position to read off the hands. If he returns too early, he merely crowds the area, making the defenders' job easier. It is a particularly good ploy to have a forward leading away from the goal square, taking his defender with him, allowing a teammate to lead into the goal square. In doing so, he gives the kicking player two target options.

Misstep

As the leading player, once you have the ball, you are in poor position, particularly forwards.

Correction

Always be aware of your position on the field and the attacking and defensive areas on the field. (See step 12 for more on team play and strategies.)

Leading Drills

It is almost impossible to practise leading by yourself. All of the following drills are to be done with a partner or in a group. Also, as proper leading requires a good kick, practising leading is also very good practice for kicking.

Most of the team kicking drills in step 5 involve leading. Rarely in a game will a ball be kicked to a stationary player. Therefore, once you have become reasonably proficient with kick-ing, drills should include kicking to a moving player.

Kicking to a player coming directly towards you is probably the easiest kick to a lead and readily practised with simple lane work. Kick the ball hard enough for the leading player to take the ball in front and well away from a defender trying to spoil. However, do not kick so hard that the receiving player does not have time to adjust should the kick be slightly off line.

Leading Drill 1. *Kick and Lead*

Face your partner from about 25 to 30 metres. As he is ready to kick, lead hard in any direction. Your partner then attempts to pass the ball to you. Do this as from a mark or free kick. Once you have the ball, your partner leads and you pass the ball to him. Both the kicker and the leader get a point if the ball is marked. The leading player loses 5 points if he drops the ball. The kicker loses 1 point if the ball cannot be marked. Vary this exercise by signalling the direction in which you will lead after a baulk. This is a competitive drill; try to score more points than your partner.

Success Check

- Time your lead so that the kicker has time to direct his kick.
- Do not lead as the kicker is going back to take his kick. Kicking from a backwards movement is rarely accurate or strong.
- Do not lead to a position that will require the kicker to change his direction drastically to get the ball to you.

Score Your Success

Score more points than your partner = 5 points

Score fewer points than your partner = 0 points

Your score ___

Leading Drill 2. *Leading and Marking*

Face your partner from about 25 to 30 metres. One player kicks to the other, who leads to mark the ball three ways: straight ahead, in a side lead and in a drop back to take the kick (preferably while moving). Have four tries at each direction, giving yourself 2 points if you mark the ball but taking off a point if you drop it. If your kick is not good enough to be marked, take a point from your score.

Success Check

- You kick the ball so it can be marked.
- Do not drop the ball. Watch it.

Score Your Success

Score 20 out of 24 points = 5 points

Score 16 to 19 points = 3 points

Score 12 to 15 points = 1 point

Your score ___

Leading Drill 3. *Competitive Kick and Lead*

Repeat the kick-and-lead drill, but this time play in pairs (figure 8.3). The kicker (K) has someone standing the mark (X), and the leading player (O) has an opponent (B) to push off from and to apply pressure.

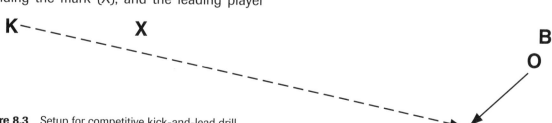

Figure 8.3 Setup for competitive kick-and-lead drill.

Success Check

- Time your lead so that the kicker has time to direct his kick.

- Do not lead as the kicker is going back to take his kick. Kicking from a backwards movement is rarely accurate or strong.

- Do not lead to a position that requires the kicker to change his direction drastically to get the ball to you.

Leading Drill 4. *Gather and Kick to the Lead*

Player A rolls or throws the ball so that player B gathers or marks the ball and then passes the ball to player C, the leading player (figure 8.4). Player C must lead to the appropriate position to receive the pass. Rotate positions after each lead so that everyone has five turns in each position.

To Increase Difficulty

- Play in pairs. Opponents provide pressure to both the kicker and the receiver.

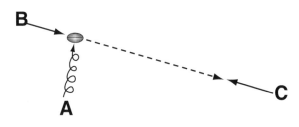

Figure 8.4 Setup for gather-and-kick-to-the-lead drill.

Success Check

- Time your lead so that you are moving and in the clear as the kicker is ready to kick, having gathered the ball.

- Lead to a position where you will be in the kicker's line of sight as he has gathered the ball and has lifted his eyes.

Score Your Success

Earn points when doing competitive leading. If as player C you were clear of the defender and in a position to take the kick without the ball being spoiled five times, give yourself 5 points. If you were clear of the defender and in position to take the kick four times, give yourself 3 points. If you were in position three times, give yourself 1 point.

Your score ___

Team Leading Drills

The distance that teams or groups are apart again depends on the size and skill of the players. There is no scoring in these drills; however, each player could give himself a subjective assessment as to how well he led and also how well he kicked. To do this, he should be aware of the success checks listed.

Team Leading Drill 1. *Threes*

Player A passes the ball to either player B or player C, who have led away from player D, who tries to intercept (figure 8.5). Once the ball is taken, the person with the ball starts the process again to players leading from the other end. Once the ball is kicked, players run through the other end and change positions so that a different player of the three becomes the interceptor.

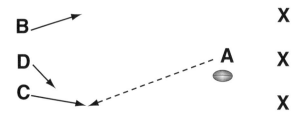

Figure 8.5 Setup for threes drill.

Success Check

- Time your lead to give the kicking player time to see you, steady and pass the ball accurately.

- Lead away from the defending partner and not across his path where he could intercept the ball.

- Run hard as you are leading and call to the kicking player as you might do in a match.

- Watch the ball and try to take it in your hands rather than on your chest.

Team Leading Drill 2. *Kick and Lead*

This drill requires four players. Player A handballs to player B and player C alternately as quickly as possible (figure 8.6). Player A chooses either player B or player C to break away and prepare to kick to player D. Once player D sees which player will be kicking, he leads to a position to receive the kick. Players change positions after each kick.

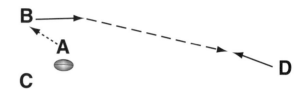

Figure 8.6 Setup for kick-and-lead team drill.

Success Check

- Watch the ball and the players handballing and be alert, ready to make your lead.

- Lead to the best position to receive the ball and where the kicking player will not have to kick across his body.

- Lead hard and fast.

GUARDING AND STANDING THE MARK

Regardless of how well a player is defended, opponents will still mark the ball during the game. At other times a free kick will be awarded. When this occurs, the defending player's aim is to prevent his opponent from playing on and by doing so give his teammates down the field time to cover their opponents. Standing the mark is a vital defensive skill that must be done well or else a 50-metre penalty could be imposed.

When a player has been awarded a mark or a free kick and an opponent unduly holds or deprives him or refuses him possession of the ball, deliberately encroaches over the mark or in any way deliberately delays the play, the spot where the mark or free kick was awarded shall be advanced not more than 50 metres nearer the goal that the player of the team entitled to the kick is attacking.

When guarding the mark, hold the player momentarily to prevent him from playing on as the mark is taken or a free kick given. If possible, place one hand on top of the ball, but do not hold it, knock it or punch it away (figure 8.7).

Figure 8.7 | **Guarding the Mark**

1. Briefly hold the player
2. Guard the ball
3. Eyes on the ball

While standing the mark, spread your arms and take a wide stance to make it more difficult for the player with the ball to play on around you (figure 8.8). Watch him because he will try to run around you if he can.

Figure 8.8 | **Standing the Mark**

1. Arms held high
2. Eyes on the opponent
3. Ready to move

On the umpire's whistle, take the position at the spot designated by the umpire and put both hands in the air so that the player has to go back and kick over them. Do not take your eyes off the player. If the opponent starts to move to either side, go to that side also and be ready for the umpire's call of 'play on', at which time you can come forwards and attempt to tackle. Between 7 and 10 seconds after a mark, the umpire will call 'play on!' at which time the defending player can go over the mark and attempt to tackle, or at the very least, harass the kicking player as he attempts to dispose of the ball, hopefully causing an error and a turnover.

Misstep

The kicker is able to play on past you on the mark.

Correction

Face the player and the ball and watch them continuously. Match the sideways movement of the kicker and do not turn side on or turn your back. Be alert for the umpire's call of 'play on'. Make the player kick over the mark by keeping your arms up while watching the ball.

Moving over the mark results in a 50-metre penalty. To avoid this penalty, know where the mark is. The umpire should identify the mark, but if you are in doubt, ask. If instructed by the umpire to come back, do so immediately with your hands raised and your eyes on the ball. Be alert for the call of 'play on', but do not anticipate and go over the mark.

If for any reason a 50-metre penalty is awarded, move back quickly, running backwards and keeping your eyes on the advancing player. He will not be allowed to play on until you are on the mark, but then be ready.

A ruckman, a rover or a follower should not have to stand the mark on a free kick. The ruck-man needs to be at the fall of the ensuing kick to fill up the space and to contest the mark. The others need to be free to follow their opponents into defence. Position players should come up from behind to stand the mark.

When there is a shot at goal, a tall player should stand the mark. He should have his arms extended up and should jump to try to block or touch the ball in flight. At the same time, another tall player (usually the ruckman) should run to the goal line to try to touch the ball as it goes through the goals or to compete in the air if the ball drops short.

Standing the Mark Drill 1. *Kick Over the Mark*

Play in pairs. Place 10 markers at various distances and angles from the goal. Each player will have one shot at goal from each of the markers. Player A takes the first kick. Player B stands the mark at the first marker with hands in the air. Player A kicks at goal over player B and gets 6 points for a goal and 1 point for a behind. Player B immediately sprints after the ball, recovers it and kicks it to player A, who has moved up to the marker. Player B runs back past player A, who handballs to player B. Player B now takes his kick for goal over player A standing the mark. Player A recov-ers the ball and passes it back to player B, who has moved to the second marker, and so on. Try to block or touch the ball that your partner kicks. Give yourself a bonus goal (6 points) if you block your partner's shot at goal.

Success Check

- Be alert for the umpire's call of 'play on'.
- Face the player and the ball and watch him continuously.

- Make the player kick over the mark by keeping your arms up while watching the ball.
- Match the sideways movement of the kicker.
- Do not turn side on or turn your back.

Standing the Mark Drill 2. *Stand the Mark*

Play in threes. Player A kicks the ball to player B and player C. Player B allows player C to mark and then stands the mark, trying to prevent player C from playing on and kicking the ball back to player A. Player B makes player C go back and kick over his mark to player A. Change roles after five kicks.

Success Check

- Face the player and the ball and watch him continuously.

- Make the player kick over the mark by keeping your arms up while watching the ball.
- Match the sideways movement of the kicker by sidestepping.
- Do not turn side on or turn your back.

Standing the Mark Drill 3. *Prevent the Play On*

Play the same way as in the stand-the-mark drill, but this time after kicking, player A runs up to try to receive a handball from player C. Player B tries to prevent the handball. Change roles after each kick.

Success Check

- Face the player and the ball and watch him continuously.
- Keep your arms up while watching the ball.

- Match the sideways movement of the kicker.
- Do not turn side on or turn your back.
- Be prepared to tackle the player who receives the ball.

LEADING, GUARDING AND STANDING THE MARK SUCCESS SUMMARY

A team streams down the field handpassing and kicking. The full forward leads powerfully from the goal square and receives an accurate pass from one of his teammates. Exhilarating stuff. It lifts the team. When shooting for goal, he kicks into the man standing the mark. Shoulders droop! Even more demoralising is when a player tries to dodge past the player standing the mark and is caught holding the ball.

Just as it is a little deflating for the player and his teammates to have a ball smothered by, or kicked into, the man on the mark, the opposite occurs for the defending team. As a result of the actions of the player standing the mark, they now have another chance to turn defence into attack. Don't ever underestimate the value of these defensive one-percenters. By being alert, holding the hands high or being prepared to tackle as soon as the kicker is called to 'play on', players standing the mark can sometimes turn the momentum of a game.

Leading Drills

1. Kick and Lead   ___ out of 5

2. Leading and Marking   ___ out of 5

4. Gather and Kick to the Lead   ___ out of 5

Standing-the-Mark Drills

1. Kick Over the Mark   ___ out of 5

2. Stand the Mark   ___ out of 5

3. Prevent the Play On   ___ out of 5

Total   ___ *out of 30*

The step you have just completed assumes that a player has marked the ball (or been given a free kick). If you have scored more than 20 out of 30 points, you are ready to move on to the next step, spoiling and smothering, in which you will try to prevent a mark being taken and an opposition player getting a clear kick away.

Spoiling and Smothering

When caught behind an opponent with less than an even chance to mark the ball, a player usually elects to spoil. In fact, a defender will almost always spoil when coming from behind his opponent to contest a ball in the air; it is simply too risky to attempt to outmark from behind.

Spoiling is the act of using a clenched fist to punch the ball away from the opponent. If the contest is near the opponent's goal, the defender will often attempt to punch the ball through the goal to concede 1 point rather than risk the ball being marked by an opposing forward and then kicked for a goal (worth 6 points).

When his opponent does mark the ball, a player tries to ensure that his opponent does not play on and has to go back and kick over the spot where the mark was taken, which is a more controlled situation for the defensive team to counter. This is called standing the mark (see step 8).

Smothering is another important defensive skill that can save goals and even games. Denying your opponents a disposal of the ball, often in a clear position of advantage, is clearly a key play. Smothering may cause a quick turnover of the ball if you can catch opposition players (who had been ready to receive the ball) out of position to defend. In such a case, a desperate defensive measure such as smothering turns defence into attack.

SPOILING

When the ball is in the air, the backman should not risk trying to outmark his opponent, especially in goal-scoring positions. If he is not certain he can take the ball, the defensive player should not attempt to take it. Instead he needs to make it as difficult as possible for his opponent to mark the ball. This is when a spoil is called for and is usually achieved by punching the ball hard.

Misstep

As the defending player, you are outmarked by an opponent.

Correction

For a defender, safety first is the key. If the forward has front position, he will likely mark the ball. Take the initiative and spoil; then try to follow up the loose ball to punch towards teammates or just to prevent the mark. It is almost a golden rule that defenders should never try to mark from behind.

In the forward lines, too, an offensive player out of position will try to bring the ball to ground to his team's advantage. This may mean a spoil to the front of the pack. If the ball is coming from defence, he may try to punch the ball back over his head in the direction of his goals. In this respect, the spoil can be an effective offensive skill, not merely a defensive one. In all of these situations, players near the spoil need to be aware of the options and take positions where they anticipate the ball will fall. When the ball is kicked in after a behind has been scored, forwards are told to keep the ball in their attacking area by spoiling the ball back towards goal. Similarly, members of the kickoff team, if forced into a position in which there will be a contested mark, will try to spoil to the boundary or, better still, back over themselves to have the ball loose and running in their attacking direction.

The spoil is as important and effective for the high ball as it is for the low ball. For the low ball, you must take care not to interfere with your opponent by reaching over his shoulder or pushing him in the back. Knowing when and how to spoil is part of being a good, disciplined defensive player.

The safety-first rule for the defensive player behind in a marking contest is that he must attempt to spoil. Players around him should know this and be ready to gather the ball as it comes to the ground. Figure 9.1 illustrates how to spoil correctly.

Figure 9.1   The Spoil

a

HIGH SPOIL
1. Eyes on the ball
2. Arm clear of the opponent
3. Clenched fist
4. High leap
5. Between the opponent's hands

b

LOW SPOIL
1. Eyes on the ball
2. Arm clear of the opponent
3. Clenched fist

c

LOW SPOIL UNDER THE ARM
1. Eyes on the ball
2. Arm clear of the opponent
3. Clenched fist
4. Between the opponent's hands

Misstep

While attempting to spoil, you don't make contact with the ball.

Correction

Failure to make contact is usually caused by poor timing of the leap and the punch. Drive your fist between the marker's hands rather than swinging from the side across the line of flight of the ball. Keep your eyes on the ball and hit through it. If the ball is not dislodged on contact, it may be because your arm is not firmly and vigorously extended.

As with marking, keep your eyes on the ball all the time during the spoil. When attempting to spoil, you must time your run and leap to get maximum height before the ball gets to the opponent's hands. Take care at all times to avoid interfering with the marking player, particularly by pushing him in the back or reaching or leaning over his shoulder.

As a spoiler, your prime objective is to prevent your opponent from marking. However, you should also be conscious of the possible options for the punched ball. You could knock the ball to a teammate. If very near the opponent's goals, you should punch the ball through the goals; in so doing, you concede a point but prevent a possible goal. As a general rule, punch the ball towards the boundary rather than into the midline of the field where it is more easily recovered and scored from by opponents.

Although spoiling is a defensive action, as a spoiler, you can take offensive advantage because you know the probable fall of the ball. You can follow up your strong action in the air by an equally strong attack on the ground to turn defence into attack.

Often a player cannot decide whether to jump and spoil because of the presence of teammates competing for the ball. In most cases, if a forward is leaping for a mark, his opponent should leap with him and attempt to spoil. This is particularly so for the backman whose opponent has a good run at the pack and a likely ride. The backman has to go with his opponent and attempt to spoil regardless of who is in front.

A skilled forward will attack the ball as if he expects to mark it. To counter this, the spoiling player must be fully committed and make a strong and hard punch. A halfhearted spoil attempt rarely succeeds.

Misstep

While attempting to spoil, you interfere with the opponent.

Correction

Time your leap. Do not put your hands on the back or shoulders of the front player to try to get height. Do not reach over his shoulders with either arm. Spoil by punching between his hands. When spoiling an attempted chest mark, spoil under the marking player's arm to eliminate the possibility of being over the shoulder.

Spoiling Drill 1. *Punch Ball High*

Hold the ball high above and in front of your head with one hand and practise the punching action of spoiling. Practise near the point post and try to punch the ball over the top of the post. Score 1 point if you do. Have 10 tries, alternating hands. Are you able to score as many with your left hand as with your right? Are you able to get to the top of the goal post?

To Decrease Difficulty

- Have a coach or a partner stand on a stool or chair and hold the ball at punching height. This can be done for young players with a number of the drills that follow.

Success Check

- Have a definite punching action using both the shoulder and elbow to provide a forceful action.
- Have a firm wrist as you make contact with the ball.
- Watch the ball.

10 spoils to the height of the point post = 5 points

Equally comfortable using either hand = 3 bonus points

Your score ___

Spoiling Drill 2.   *Punch Ball Angles*

Hold the ball at different angles to represent the spoil from chest marks. Perform the drill at the kickoff line and try to get the ball over the goal line. Score 1 point if you do. Have 10 tries, alternating hands. Are you able to score as many with your left hand as with your right?

Success Check

- Have a definite punching action using both the shoulder and elbow to provide a forceful action.

- Have a firm wrist as you make contact with the ball.
- Watch the ball.

Score Your Success

10 spoils to the goal line = 5 points

Equally comfortable using either hand = 3 bonus points

Your score ___

Spoiling Drill 3.   *Partner Punch*

Perform the punch-ball drills (spoiling drills 1 and 2) again, but compete with a partner. First have your partner hold the ball high above and in front of your head. He may stand on a chair or stool to give a more realistic height. Experiment with this to get the height right before you start scoring. Jump and punch the ball. Practise near the point post and try to punch the ball over the top of the post. Score 1 point if you do. Have 10 tries, alternating hands. Switch roles with your partner.

Now have your partner hold the ball at different angles to represent the spoil from chest marks. Punch the ball. Perform the drill at the kickoff line and try to get the ball over the goal line. Score 1 point if you do. Have 10 tries, alternating hands. Switch roles with your partner.

Success Check

- Have a few tries standing and then practise leaping and punching the ball.
- Time your punch with your leap.

- Have a definite punching action using both the shoulder and elbow to provide a forceful action.
- Have a firm wrist as you make contact with the ball.
- Watch the ball.

Score Your Success

10 spoils to the height of the point post = 5 points

8 or 9 spoils to the height of the point post = 3 points

6 or 7 spoils to the height of the point post = 1 point

10 spoils to the goal line = 5 points

8 or 9 spoils to the goal line = 3 points

6 or 7 spoils to the goal line = 1 point

Your score ___

Spoiling Drill 4. *Leap and Spoil*

Play in groups of three. Player A stands in front of player B and player C and throws the ball high into the air. Player B and player C compete against each other, with one being the designated marker and the other the spoiler. Have five tries each at marking and spoiling. Players get 2 points for every spoil but lose 1 point each time their opponent marks the ball. Lose 2 points for each free kick awarded by the throwing player against the spoiler for over-the-shoulder or in-the-back penalties.

Success Check

- Time your leap to be at maximum height as you spoil.

- Punch your fist between the hands of the marking player.
- Try to have your punching action angle directly opposite that of the incoming ball.
- Use good timing.

Score Your Success

Score 8 points or more = 5 points

Score 6 or 7 points = 3 points

Score 4 or 5 points = 1 point

Your score ____

Spoiling Drill 5. *Chest Mark Spoil*

Play in groups of three. Player A stands in front of player B and player C and throws the ball at the chest of the leading player. Player B and player C compete against each other, with one being the designated marker and the other the spoiler. Have five tries each at marking and spoiling. Players get 2 points for every spoil but lose 1 point each time their opponent marks the ball. Lose 2 points for each free kick awarded by the throwing player against the spoiler for over-the-shoulder or in-the-back penalties. The player throwing the ball acts as the umpire and awards 'free kicks' for infringements.

Success Check

- Time your leap to be at maximum height as you spoil.
- Punch your fist between the hands of the marking player.
- Do not push your opponent in the back or reach over his shoulder.

Score Your Success

Score 8 points or more = 5 points

Score 6 or 7 points = 3 points

Score 4 or 5 points = 1 point

Your score ____

Spoiling Drill 6. *End-to-End Spoil*

Practise end-to-end kicking in pairs, with the player being caught behind attempting to spoil. Each spoil earns 1 point.

Success Check

- Time your leap.
- Do not give away free kicks.
- Punch the ball well away from the marking competition.

Score Your Success

Score more points than your partner = 5 points

Score fewer points than your partner = 0 points

Your score ____

Spoiling Drill 7. *Team Spoil*

In groups of six, work together in two teams of three. Two are at one end acting as spoiler and crumber. (The player who positions himself to gather the falling ball is often described as gathering crumbs.) The third man is 25 to 30 metres away and acts as kicker and marker (figure 9.2). Your opponents do the same. The ball is kicked high and two players contest the mark and spoil, with the spoiling player trying to get the ball to his teammate on the ground. Talk to your teammate to decide where he is going to try to spoil the ball. Teams score 2 points when they recover the ball but lose 1 when their opponents mark the ball. Rotate the positions after every five kicks to your team.

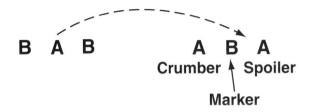

Figure 9.2 Setup for team-spoil drill.

Success Check

- Time your leap.
- Do not give away free kicks.
- Hit the ball in the direction of your on-ground partner.

Score Your Success

Outscore your opponents = 5 points

Your score ___

Spoiling Drill 8. *Funnel Ball*

This drill encourages aggressive running and holding your position as well as hand, chest or overhead marking and spoiling.

Mark a funnel out with cones (figure 9.3). Players A, B and C are behind a restraining line about 5 metres from the entrance to the funnel. They can be standing or lying either on their fronts or backs in a row. When the coach calls 'go', they regain their feet and race for the entrance to the funnel. (Because he is nearest the funnel, player B should be in front, although not necessarily.) As the first person enters the funnel, the coach throws or handballs the ball so that it can be taken either in the hands or on the chest or overhead.

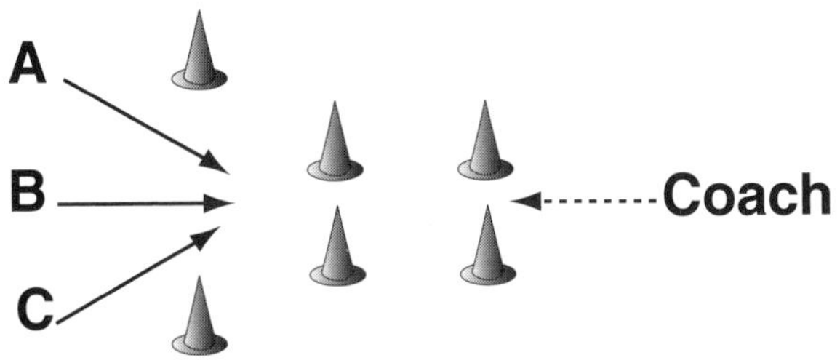

The second player into the funnel tries to spoil. If the mark is successful, the player handballs the ball back to the coach and the third player runs through for a return handpass. Players return to the restraining line and rotate positions. Have five tries each position.

Success Check

- React quickly to the starting signal.
- Spoil to the side or under the arms and not over the shoulders.
- Take care not to give away any free kicks.

Score Your Success

As the spoiler:

Spoil the ball 4 or 5 times out of 5 attempts = 5 points

Spoil the ball 2 or 3 times out of 5 attempts = 3 points

Spoil the ball 1 time out of 5 attempts = 1 point

Your score ___

Figure 9.3 Setup for funnel-ball drill.

SMOTHERING

Often taken as a measure of a player's desperation, the smother is an attempt to block the ball off the foot of an opponent in the act of kicking. A smother is usually attempted when the defensive player is out of position to attempt a tackle or bump and therefore tries the only move available to nullify the kick.

Although smothering appears difficult and dangerous, if properly executed, it is very effective and has minimal risk to the smotherer. Indecision is the main cause of problems in attempting to smother. In smothering, timing is vital in that your hands must be over the ball at the right time. It is here that indecision will lead to late positioning.

The smother is generally made from the side or the front with the fingers spread and the thumbs close together or overlapping. The arms are close together and stretched but relaxed so that they can absorb the impact of the kicked ball.

To smother, position yourself close to the player (figure 9.4). Place your hands in the anticipated path of the ball as it leaves the player's foot. Your palms face the ball. The closer to the foot the smother is made, the better and safer it will be. Your arms protect your face and stop the free swing of the kicker's leg. Keep your eyes on the ball and your head down.

| Figure 9.4 | Smothering the Ball |

a

PREPARATION

1. Fingers spread
2. Palms turned towards the ball
3. Arms, wrists and thumbs close together
4. Hands ready for the ball
5. Head down
6. Eyes on the ball
7. Body crouched

b

c

EXECUTION

1. Fingers spread
2. Palms turned towards the ball
3. Arms, wrists and thumbs close together
4. Hands close to the foot
5. Head down
6. Eyes on the ball
7. Body crouched

FOLLOW-THROUGH

1. Recover the ball

A handball can also be smothered. The same principles apply when smothering a ball in the hands as apply when smothering a kick.

When the kicker is still able to get the ball away, usually it is because the player attempting to smother the ball is afraid of being hit by the ball. The player's head is turned away from the ball and he is trying to smother from too far away from the kicker's foot. A good, safe smother is accomplished by keeping the eyes on the ball, the body close to the ball and the arms close together with palms over the ball near the kicker's foot. To get into this position, the smotherer needs to bend at the knees and hips and have good timing. As with many other techniques of football, a decisive movement is essential. Indecision leads to failure.

A common habit when attempting to smother is to bring the hands down in a swatting action to block the ball. This does not make the smother any more effective but does make missing the ball more likely.

A good exercise is to try competitive drills such as 'keep the ball away', two-on-two, or handball football, in which tackling is not allowed but smothering is.

Smothering Drill. *The Smother*

The smother can be practised by player A hand-passing the ball to player B, who moves in to kick while player C comes from the side to attempt to smother (figure 9.5). The angle of player C's approach should vary. This exercise should be done first with the kicker stationary and then with the kicker moving to take the ball and kick. Change positions after each kick and have five attempts each to smother the kick from a stationary player and five from a moving player.

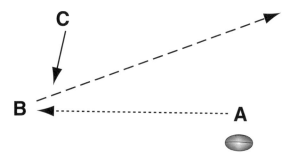

Figure 9.5 Setup for the smother drill.

SPOILING AND SMOTHERING SUCCESS SUMMARY

Perhaps surprisingly, the defensive skills of spoiling and smothering do not show up often in a game. It would be unusual for a team to accumulate more than 15 spoils and 5 smothers in a game. Because of this, many players assume that these skills are not important and spend little time practising them. Young players particularly fall into this error; younger players see the marks, kicks and handballs as more important. However, the player who is skilled in these aspects of the game can play a significant role in saving a game by a desperate goal-line spoil or courageous smother. All players need to know not only the value of these skills but also how to perform them in a game. A player never knows when these skills might make him a hero.

Two heroes in recent games have been St. Kilda's Luke Penny and Port Adelaide's Byron Pickett.

During round 2, 2005, in the last seconds of a game that had been touch and go all day, the ball was kicked high into Fremantle's goal square. Their ever-reliable Mark Pavlich stood under the ball ready to mark and then kick the winning goal. As he took off, out of nowhere came Luke Penny, who leaped and drove his fist into the ball. The siren sounded. St. Kilda won by 2 points.

During round 10, 2004, Geelong's Josh Hunt was looking for a chip kick away from half back as the Cats were working a routine kick-in after Port Adelaide forward Josh Mahoney missed a shot at goal. Byron Pickett's full-stretched smother pushed the ball to Brendon Lade, whose long handpass to Mahoney left the power forward to run towards the southern goal at AAMI Stadium without an opponent. His goal, with 45 seconds to play, set up Port's stunning 4-point win in an epic game.

Spoiling Drills

1. Punch Ball High   ___ out of 5

2. Punch Ball Angles   ___ out of 5

3. Partner Punch   ___ out of 10

4. Leap and Spoil   ___ out of 5

5. Chest Mark Spoil   ___ out of 5

6. End-to-End Spoil   ___ out of 5

7. Team Spoil   ___ out of 5

8. Funnel Ball   ___ out of 5

Smothering Drill

1. The Smother   ___ out of 5

Total   ___ **out of 50**

If you scored at least 40 points, you have done well. If you scored 50 points or more, you are on your way to becoming a hero—only on your way, though! Now you ARE on your way to step 10, ruckwork.

Ruckwork

Ruckwork is the contesting of a ball that has been either bounced or thrown up by the umpire. The objective is to tap the ball in the air to a teammate. Ruckwork is done to start the game, to begin each quarter or to restart after each goal.

Ruckwork is also done when the umpire wishes to clear a scrimmage or when the ball is disputed with no player having clear possession. Ruckmen compete for the ball from a throw-in when a boundary umpire returns the ball into play after it has gone out of bounds. For both of these situations, there are no restrictions on the distance and direction of the ruckmen's approach.

In junior football the central umpire can nominate any two players to contest the ball up, so every player will need to know and to practise the basic techniques of ruckwork. In senior football, however, ruckwork is the province of the taller, larger players, called *ruckmen*.

The ruckman's objective is to get the disputed ball to a teammate who will be in position either to run away with it or to dispose of it by handball or kick to his team's advantage. This is sometimes called *getting first use of the ball*. Any player may use the rucking technique to get the ball to advantage if it is bouncing high or if he is not in a position to mark, although usually when this occurs, it is surer to take the bouncing ball in both hands and handball to a teammate.

In senior football there is a 10-metre-diameter circle around the spot where the umpire will bounce or throw up the ball to start the game each quarter and restart the game after each goal. Both ruckmen must have both feet within that circle as the ball is bounced or thrown up. This new ruckwork law (2005) is not used universally in junior, school and amateur football, but is left to the discretion of the controlling body. For the purpose of this step, we have chosen not to include it.

RUCKING

Figure 10.1 illustrates the important factors in making a success in ruckwork, whether the contest takes place at the centre bounce or at a boundary throw-in.

A Legend in the Making?

Ruckwork is the domain of big men. Many big men have become legends of the game, not only for their ruckwork but also because they have been larger-than-life characters. A legend who exemplified what ruckwork is about is West Australia's Graham Farmer. His tap-outs were attacking and revolutionised the game. Very adept at palming the ball to his smaller teammates, Farmer placed his own individual stamp on the game by taking the ball out of the air and using his brilliant handballing skills to get it to a teammate well in the clear, something that the present rules would not allow.

By comparison, Brisbane's Clark Keating's reputation is not legendary, but his almost faultless display of ruckwork in the 2003 Grand Final made him a contender for the Norm Smith Medal on that day. He would have been a worthy winner, having used all the rucking skills expected of great exponents of the art of rucking. Long punches towards goal, accurately palming the ball to either side, flips back over the head from boundary throw-ins all gave his on-ballers and position players first look at and use of the ball. Because he was not predictable, his opponents could not anticipate and work off his dominance. Added to this was his reading of the play and his positioning himself around the field to his team's advantage. His was the almost perfect example to ruckmen of all ages as to how to play the role.

The result? A third Premiership Medallion around his neck. A legend in the making perhaps?

Figure 10.1   Ruckwork

a

BALL UP

1. Eyes on the ball
2. Leap off one foot
3. Bend the knee of the other leg
4. Open the hand
5. High ball contact

b

THROW-IN

1. Eyes on the ball
2. Two-foot takeoff
3. Open the hand
4. High ball contact
5. Use the hand closest to the opponent
6. Body against the opponent

Remember that it is easier to direct the ball with your fingers and palm than with your fist. If the ball does not go to the target player, tell the target player to go to the spot most comfortable for you to direct the ball. Generally this direction is communicated using a clock face; for example, 'stand at 10 o'clock'. The target player should call for the ball and you should aim for his voice.

As with any ball skill, keeping your eyes on the ball is vital. When confronted directly by the opposition ruckman, you may be tempted to look at him rather than at the ball. Resist this temptation and keep your eyes on the ball. Learn and practise the fundamentals of rucking.

Use both your arms and your legs to get height. Generally, leap off one foot (the foot opposite the hand that is reaching for the ball). Bend the other leg for lift and to offer protection from body contact. Many ruckmen wear shin guards to protect their legs because of the contact in ruck contests.

Time your leap so that you contact the ball as high as possible. Be aware, however, that the ball may not bounce straight up. When it doesn't, you must be ready to make adjustments in your movement and timing.

The open hand is more accurate than a closed fist for palming the ball to a waiting teammate. Even greater accuracy is achieved by using your fingertips rather than the flat of your hand. Direction is achieved by turning your wrist so that your hand is facing the direction in which you want the ball to go. On some odd occasions, such as an errant bounce or a boundary throw-in, the ruckman may find himself under little pressure from the opposing ruckman. In such cases, he can accurately direct the ball with both hands to his waiting teammates on the ground.

When trying to hit for distance rather than accuracy (as when trying to clear the ball away from a congested area or defensively through the goals or towards the boundary), punch the ball with a clenched fist in much the same fashion as spoiling a mark.

When both you and an opposing ruckman are approaching the ball from the same direction (as for throw-ins and as is allowed for by the rules for ball ups other than in the centre circle), use the hand closest to your opponent. If possible, use both hands if you are trying to bring the ball down in front of you.

Make sure that your teammates know where you are trying to hit the ball (see step 12 on team play). They should call to you, and you will need to hit to the vocal target and to a prearranged position. Your eyes should be on the ball.

There are several approaches to the ball and opponent in ruckwork (figure 10.2). At a centre bounce at the start of each quarter and after each goal, the ruckmen must approach each other from either side of the line drawn across the centre circle.

Players will generally approach each other straight on (figure 10.2a), but this will vary depending on tactics and the relative sizes of the contesting ruckmen (players may come from a different angle to counter larger, dominant ruckmen) (figure 10.2b). Often a smaller ruckman will try to manoeuvre to come in from the side of his opponent (figure 10.2c), much like the tactic used for a boundary throw-in in which the players are most likely to be side by side (figure 10.3). The larger ruckman then understandably may adjust to come straight on again (figure 10.2d).

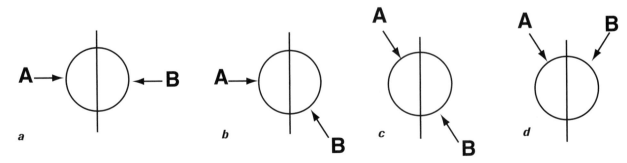

Figure 10.2 Centre bounce approach options: *(a)* straight on; *(b)* coming from an angle to counter a larger ruckman; *(c)* a smaller ruckman coming from the side; *(d)* a larger ruckman adjusting to come straight on.

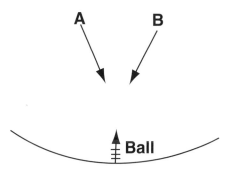

Figure 10.3 Boundary throw-in.

Misstep

You are beaten to the ball by the opposing ruckman.

Correction

You may be mistiming the leap or not reaching to the full height of the ball. Make sure your eyes are on the ball and not on your opponent and that you leap from one foot only, the foot opposite the palming hand. If you are smaller than your opponent, do not try to body him. Instead try to get a clear leap at the ball.

Ruckwork Drill 1. *Target Rucking*

By yourself, throw the ball into the air and leap, attempting to palm it to imaginary teammates. Place five markers (hoops or cones) about you and try to direct the ball to them. Number the markers and try to hit each in turn before progressing to the next one.

Success Check

- Use your knee to help you get height in your leap.
- Watch the ball at all times.

- Use your fingers and palms to direct the ball.

Score Your Success

Hit each target in succession with no misses = 5 points

Hit each target in 6 to 8 attempts = 3 points

Hit each target in 9 or 10 attempts = 1 point

Your score ___

Ruckwork Drill 2. *Partner Ruckwork*

A partner tosses the ball into the air and you try to hit it back to him. Add difficulty by having your partner toss the ball and then move and call for you to hit the ball to him. Have five turns and change over.

Success Check

- Keep your eyes on the ball.
- Listen for your partner's voice, which becomes the target.

- Time your leap to hit the ball while you are in the air.

Score Your Success

Return the ball to your partner five out of five attempts = 5 points

Return the ball to your partner four out of five attempts = 3 points

Return the ball to your partner three out of five attempts = 1 point

Your score ___

113

Ruckwork Drill 3. *Ruck Shootout*

In pairs, use the five targets you used in ruckwork drill 1, target rucking. Place them about 2 metres from where the ball will be thrown up at 12, 3, 6 and 9 o'clock and one several metres beyond the 12 o'clock marker (figure 10.4). This last one is called 'Big Ben'. Just before he throws the ball up, your partner randomly calls out the target you are to try to hit. Have 10 tries and change over. Who scored the most hits out of 10?

Success Check

- Direct the ball to the correct target.
- Watch the ball and leap high.
- Time your leap to hit the ball from as high as possible.

Score Your Success

Hit 8 to 10 targets in 10 attempts = 5 points

Hit 6 or 7 targets in 10 attempts = 3 points

Hit 4 or 5 targets in 10 attempts = 1 point

Your score ___

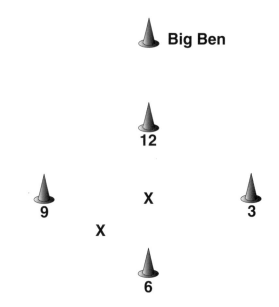

Figure 10.4   Setup for ruck-shootout drill.

Ruckwork Drill 4. *Boundary Throw-In Hit to the Call*

This drill requires three players. Player A throws the ball in from the boundary. Player B (the ruck-man) tries to hit it back to player C, who is calling for the ball from a different position for each throw-in (figure 10.5). Have five tries in each role, changing over after every five attempts.

Success Check

- Direct the ball to the voice target.
- Run in a couple of steps, watch the ball and leap high.
- Time your leap to hit the ball from as high as possible.

Score Your Success

As the ruckman, successfully hit the ball to your target five out of five attempts = 5 points

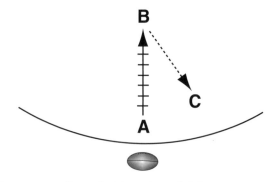

Figure 10.5   Setup for hit-to-the-call drill.

As the ruckman, successfully hit the ball back to your target four out of five attempts = 3 points

As the ruckman, successfully hit the ball back to your target three out of five attempts = 1 point

Your score ___

Ruckwork Drill 5. *Competitive Ruckwork*

Play with two partners about the same size. Player A throws the ball up for player B and player C to contest. Both player B and player C try to get the ball back to player A, who has moved back from the toss-up and calls for the ball. Change over roles after each contest so that you are not competing against the same opponent all the time. Have five attempts each. Score 1 point for each successful attempt in getting the ball back to the throwing player.

To Increase Difficulty

- Repeat the drill, but this time, instead of doing the ball-up competition, have the person throw in the ball from the boundary so that the ruckmen compete side by side for the ball.

Success Check

- Direct the ball to the voice target.
- Vary the direction of your run-up.
- Run in a couple of steps, watch the ball and leap high.
- Time your leap to hit the ball from as high as possible.

Score Your Success

As the ruckman, successfully hit the ball back five out of five attempts = 5 points

As the ruckman, successfully hit the ball back four out of five attempts = 3 points

As the ruckman, successfully hit the ball back three out of five attempts = 1 point

Your score ___

Ruckwork Drill 6. *Competitive Ruckwork With Targets*

This drill is the same as competitive ruckwork, but this time with a target for each player to try to hit (figure 10.6). Have five contests each, changing after each so that you are not competing against the same player all the time or aiming at the same target. Score 1 point if you win the ruck contest and another 3 points if you hit the target.

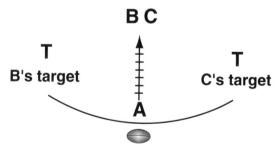

Figure 10.6 Setup for competitive-ruckwork-with-targets drill.

Success Check

- Try to get higher than your opponent to get your hand to the ball first.
- Watch the ball.
- Are you able to leap off the other leg and use the other hand to palm the ball?

Score Your Success

12 to 15 points = 5 points

10 or 11 points = 3 points

8 or 9 points = 1 point

Your score ___

TEAM RUCKWORK DRILLS

Many team drills can incorporate or substitute ruckwork, particularly the off-hands drills. In these cases the ball can be thrown into the air by a coach to simulate a ruck contest. Teams today usually have a ruck bag for ruckmen to jump into rather than an opposition player at practice. This gives practising ruckmen con-fidence to leap at the ball without the fear of being injured and encourages them to use the knee not only to leap high but also to use an opponent to get higher. However, this is more in keeping with senior football and should not be encouraged with young players.

Team Ruckwork Drill 1. *Centre or In-Field Bounce*

A coach throws the ball up in the centre circle. Player R runs in, leaps on the ruck bag and palms the ball to either player A or player B, who have been positioned to take the ball according to team strategy. Once player A or player B has the ball, he kicks it to the lead of player C, who is being pursued by player D.

Success Check

- Know the team decision or strategy as to where the ball is to be hit. The ruckman needs to talk to his receivers to clarify this.
- Leap high, watch the ball and direct the ball down to the designated player.
- Player C, who doesn't know who is going to get the ball, holds his lead and then runs hard to an appropriate position to receive the ball.

Team Ruckwork Drill 2. *Boundary Throw-In*

The ball is thrown in from the boundary. Player R palms it down to player A or player B, who are positioned according to team strategy (figure 10.7). If player A gets the ball, he kicks it to player D, who has led from the goal square. If the ball goes to player B, he passes it down the boundary to player C, who has led.

To Increase Difficulty

- Identify specific positions to which the ball is to be hit—down, forwards, to the side, behind.

- Have the two players who are competing against each other for the knock offer only token opposition.
- Increase the amount of opposition.
- Have the ruckmen work as a team with one of the players on the ground.

Success Check

- The group of players work efficiently as a team dependent on to whom the ruckman has directed the ball.

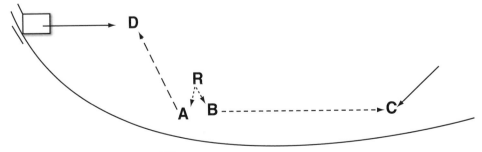

Figure 10.7 Setup for boundary-throw-in drill.

RUCKWORK SUCCESS SUMMARY

Although ruckwork is the province of the big man, an understanding of ruckwork is a requirement of all players, even though most will never leap into a ruck contest. Unlike most team games, in Australian football teams are rarely guaranteed possession of the ball to start or restart a game. Teams will develop dead-ball strategies based around ruckmen competing for the ball (see step 12). The players around the ruck contest, both set position players and on-ballers, will need to know the team strategies, know the strengths and weaknesses of their ruckman (and indeed the opposition's ruckman) and communicate with him in attempting to gain possession of the ball. Coaches who specialise in ruckwork will work with their ruckmen and midfield players to sharpen the ruckmen's skills but also to hone the team disciplines and strategies of those working with him.

Ruckwork Drills

1. Target Rucking	___ out of 5
2. Partner Ruckwork	___ out of 5
3. Ruck Shootout	___ out of 5
4. Boundary Throw-In Hit to the Call	___ out of 5
5. Competitive Ruckwork	___ out of 5
6. Competitive Ruckwork With Targets	___ out of 5
Total	___ *out of 30*

Ruckwork involves body-on-body competition and sometimes quite dramatic impact. Because Australian football is a contact game, all players will at times have to commit to a clash of bodies during a game. The next step (bumping, pushing and shepherding) will look at how these forms of contact can be used to put pressure on opposition players but also to take it off teammates.

For a ruckman, 25 out of 30 points is a good score and should be achievable with practice. For others, a score of 15 will show that you have some understanding of what rucking involves. Now all players will need to get involved in the next step: bumping, pushing and shepherding.

117

Bumping, Pushing and Shepherding

The laws of Australian football allow players to push or bump other players, but there are restrictions as to how and when this can be done. A player may be fairly met by an opponent by the use of hip, shoulder, chest, arms or open hands provided the player either has the ball or is not more than 5 metres away from the ball. However, a free kick will be awarded against a player who pushes, bumps or shepherds an opponent who is in the air attempting to mark. Any bump, hit or push to the head will result in a free kick against the offending player and, if deemed intentional or reckless, may result in the player being reported for misconduct or rough play. The player may face sanctions. A player also may not charge another even though the contact may be within 5 metres of the ball. In general terms, charging is defined as colliding with an opposition player with unreasonable or unnecessary force or when the contacted player is not in the immediate contest for the football and not reasonably expecting such contact.

Usually, when a player has possession of the ball, you should tackle him. However, there are occasions when you may be better off bumping the ball carrier instead, such as when he is in the act of kicking or handballing and he is just out of reach to wrap your arms about him.

The most effective bump or push is made on an unsuspecting opponent or one who is already off balance. In these cases your bump will knock the ball loose and you or a teammate will likely be able to gather it. If a player does not yet possess the ball and it is being contested, then a bump can be a very effective means of taking the player out of the play.

An alert and effective piece of teamwork is to solidly bump an opponent who is pursuing a teammate (remember that the ball must be within 5 metres at the time). This is a form of *shepherding* and is an important team skill. The player attempts to check or block the approach or tackle of an opponent so that a teammate may take possession of the ball and then dispose of it under less pressure. That is the ultimate objective in shepherding—to take pressure off the teammate. It is an important tactic to help a teammate who is being closely tagged. Handball the ball to your teammate and then follow the ball past him and bump the tagging opponent.

BUMPING AND PUSHING

Bumping requires an aggressive approach and a well-timed hit. As shown in figure 11.1, you should bunch yourself up by tucking your arm to your side with your elbow close to your hip and by lifting your shoulder to your chin. Bend your knees slightly to get added stability. Deliver the bump with your shoulder, hip or both.

Figure 11.1   Bumping

1. Arm tucked to the side
2. Elbow to the side
3. Chin and shoulder tucked
4. Knees bent
5. Feet spread
6. Push off on the outside leg

Misstep

While bumping, you become unbalanced.

Correction

Keep both feet on the ground, preferably wide apart with your knees bent. The bump is most effective if the opponent is already off balance or not expecting to be bumped. In most cases it is safer and more effective to tackle the player if he has the ball.

When attempting to bump, keep both feet on the ground. Otherwise, you might take yourself out of the play along with your opponent. You may deliver a bump to the side or front of the player, but not to the back or the head nor while he is in the air attempting a mark.

Push (figure 11.2) only when you can't get close enough to tackle your opponent or if he is about to dispose of the ball. The push can be to the side or the chest only and must be done with open hands. You need to take care when pushing to the side as this is easily interpreted as a push in the back and a free kick might be given.

Figure 11.2 | Pushing

1. Hands open
2. Elbows bent
3. Push to the side
4. Feet spread for balance

SHEPHERDING

Shepherding can be achieved by bumping, but even more common is to position yourself between the attacking opponent and your teammate, thus checking the opponent's movement.

Shepherding is even more effective if you spread your arms and stick your rump back into the approaching player (figure 11.3).

Figure 11.3 | Shepherding

a

b

PREPARATION

1. Arms extended
2. Feet spread
3. Body low

EXECUTION

1. Lean into the opponent
2. Knees bent

Misstep

The opponent breaks through or avoids the shepherd.

Correction

Know where the opponent is either by watching or keeping your body against his and move to ensure that you are always between him and your teammate. Shepherding takes strength; any looseness in the arm position or body action will allow the opponent past. Spread and firmly position your feet, brace your body and push back hard against your opponent.

Move into a position between the opponent and your teammate. As the opponent moves, you move also, always trying to stay between the opponent and your teammate. Talk to your teammate to inform him of any pressure he is under from a would-be tackler and how much time he has to dispose of the ball.

A shepherd, particularly when done in a stationary position as when a teammate is picking up a ball or is about to mark, requires firmness or the tackler will easily break through. Extend your arms strongly and spread out your feet. Always know where your opponent is, either by watching him or feeling his body against yours. Keep low and lean back into him to hold your ground and not let him brush past you. Do not hold him in any way, particularly by curling your arms around him as this will result in a free kick for the opposition, as will a shepherd when the ball is more than 5 metres away.

On occasion it is necessary to shepherd the ball rather than a teammate. For instance, when the ball is rolling or going between the goal posts for a goal, you risk being tackled and losing the ball if you try to pick it up. You will also shepherd the ball if an opponent is trying to touch it as it goes through the goals either on the ground or in the air. The principles here are the same as when shepherding a player, but it is probably more important to spread your feet, crouch a little lower and hold your ground.

When shepherding, be careful not to interfere with the opponent. Remember, a player cannot be bumped or shepherded if he is attempting to mark or if he is not within 5 metres of the ball. You may bump only in the side or the front below the shoulders. When bumping, keep your elbows close to your sides.

During practice it is valuable to work on handballing to a teammate and then running after him with your arms wide out so that an imaginary opponent would have difficulty getting past you to apply a tackle. Drills that are used for running and baulking are also worthwhile for practising tackling and bumping.

Bumping, Pushing and Shepherding Drill 1. *Protect the Ball*

Play with a partner. Put a ball on the ground about 5 metres from both of you. One player protects the ball from the other by shepherding. This drill can be made competitive by having someone time you to see how long you can stop your opponent from touching the ball. Change over. Have two tries each.

Success Check

- Spread your feet and bend your knees to create greater stability.
- Back into your opponent. Know where he is at all times.

- Move with your opponent by sidestepping.
- Always face the ball.

Score Your Success

Prevent your partner from touching the ball for longer than 30 seconds = 5 points

Prevent your partner from touching the ball for 20 to 29 seconds = 3 points

Prevent your partner from touching the ball for 10 to 19 seconds = 1 point

Your score ___

Bumping, Pushing and Shepherding Drill 2. *One on Three*

This drill requires four players. Three players form a triangle and link hands (figure 11.4). Player A has to catch player B by trying to get around player C and player D. Player C and player D move to bump player A and shepherd player B. Player A cannot go across the triangle or break the grip. Each player has one minute to be the chaser.

Success Check

- The protected player is not touched.
- The defending players move sideways easily in both directions.
- When in position to do so, defending players give a hip and shoulder bump to the chasing player as he tries to get past them.

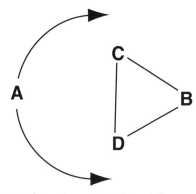

Figure 11.4 Setup for one-on-three drill.

Bumping, Pushing and Shepherding Drill 3. *Protect the Tail*

Play with four players. Players A, B and C form a line with player A facing players B and C. Player B puts his hands on player A's hips, and player C holds player B's hips. Player D tries to get around players A and B to catch player C (figure 11.5). Player A shepherds. Play for one minute; then change over.

Success Check

- The protected player is not touched.
- The defending players move sideways easily in both directions.
- Player A keeps between the chasing and target players.

Score Your Success

The player you protect is not touched by the chasing player = 5 points

Your score ___

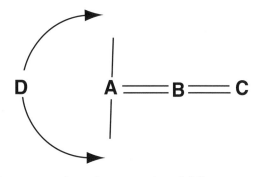

Figure 11.5 Setup for protect-the-tail drill.

Bumping, Pushing and Shepherding Drill 4. *Protect the Runner*

Players A, B and C stand 1 metre apart (figure 11.6). Player A has the ball. On the signal all players sprint to the marker 20 metres away; player A has to bounce the ball at least once. Player B has to shepherd player A by blocking player C, who is trying to catch player A. Vary the drill by starting with player A sitting, player B kneeling and player C standing. The signal to start can be the ball being handballed to player A. Players A, B and C each take three turns at shepherding.

Success Check

- Be aware of where the chasing player is as he may dodge to try to get past.

- Keep your arms spread to make yourself difficult to get past.
- Continually move to be between the chaser and the ball carrier.

Score Your Success

As player B, prevent player C from catching player A three times = 5 points

As player B, prevent player C from catching player A two times = 3 points

As player B, prevent player C from catching player A one time = 1 point

Your score ____

Because the objective in shepherding is to protect a teammate from being tackled by opposition players, it stands to reason that many of the drills used to practise tackling can with some modification be used to include shepherding.

Team Shepherding Drill 1. *One (Plus One)-on-One Competitive*

The coach stands in front of a group of three players. The middle player, player B, is the shepherder. The coach randomly kicks, throws or rolls the ball towards the first group, slightly favouring one of the outside players. This player attacks the ball, gathers and attempts to get it back to the coach by handballing. The other outside player becomes the tackler and attempts to tackle player A as he gathers the ball or attempts to handball. The middle player, player B, tries to protect player A by blocking and shepherding. Football rules apply. Players rotate positions after every try. Have five tries each position.

Success Check

- Be aware of where the chasing player is as he may dodge to try to get past.
- Keep your arms spread to make yourself difficult to get past.
- Continually move to be between the chaser and the ball carrier.

Score Your Success

As player B, prevent player C from catching player A five times = 5 points

As player B, prevent player C from catching player A four times = 3 points

As player B, prevent player C from catching player A three times = 1 point

Your score ____

Team Shepherding Drill 2. *One on Two*

In a fairly restricted area the coach kicks the ball high to players A and B, who work as a team to take the ball, with one blocking, and then run the ball back and handball to the coach. Both must touch the ball at least once before it goes back to the coach. Player C tries to intercept the ball or to tackle the ball carrier. Players A and B protect each other by shepherding. Only forward ball movement is allowed.

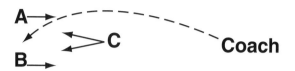

Figure 11.6 Setup for protect-the-runner drill.

To Increase Difficulty

• Require three touches before the ball is handballed to the coach.

Success Check

• Follow up your handball with a shepherd or bump to protect your teammate.

Team Shepherding Drill 3. *Four-on-Four and Shoot for Goal*

In a 10-metre-square area about 20 metres from goal, two teams of four players play keep the ball away using handballs, shepherds, blocks and tackles. On a signal from the coach, the team who is in possession of the ball at the time has a shot at goal.

Success Check

• All handballs, shepherds, blocks and tackles are legal.

• Apply pressure when the opposition has the ball.

• Protect teammates when they have the ball.

Score Your Success

Have 10 competitions—that is, 10 shots at goal. The team that scores the most goals wins.

Your team wins = 5 points

Your score ___

BUMPING, PUSHING AND SHEPHERDING SUCCESS SUMMARY

Time and space are the essence of most team games: Players need time to do something with the ball with minimal pressure and maximal space. Shepherding provides a teammate just a little bit more time and a little less pressure to dispose of the ball effectively. Bumping and pushing are legitimate ways to harass players with or without the ball (to use either, the player must be within 5 metres of the ball), particularly as they are about to gain possession of the ball. Once a player has the ball, though, you should almost always try to tackle rather than bump or push.

Bumping, Pushing and Shepherding Drills

    1. Protect the Ball   ___ out of 5

    3. Protect the Tail   ___ out of 5

    4. Protect the Runner   ___ out of 5

Team Shepherding Drills

    1. One (Plus One)-on-One Competitive   ___ out of 5

    3. Four-on-Four and Shoot for Goal   ___ out of 5

Total   ___ *out of 25*

Most bumping, pushing and shepherding practice is done in a team situation and is not easily scored. The score you have achieved in the drills in this step will give you only an indication of how effectively you perform the drills. What will be more of a guide is how well you perform these skills in group situations and how you mark off the success checks, particularly when you are under pressure.

Now that you have gone through the steps of understanding, practising and achieving some degree of skill in the various aspects of Australian football, it is time to put those skills into the game situation. The next step, team tactics and strategies, sets about doing just that.

Team Tactics and Strategies

One of the exciting aspects of Australian football is its continual ebb and flow. The ball moves quickly from defence into attack and back again equally quickly. Consequently, players need to be versatile, able to play both offence and defence.

Not so long ago youngsters learning the wing or centre positions were told that these positions were very difficult because they required both attacking and defending. This is still the case, but now this emphasis is placed on *all* players in *all* positions.

Many of the best attacking moves originate from the last line of defence. Even forward players need to be aware of defence to prevent opponents from mounting an offensive move after gaining possession deep in their own defensive area. It is not unusual for a side to have a good win with their full back or back pocket playing a dominant role. Similarly, forward players often are commended for their team play, not for kicking goals but for fighting desperately to keep the ball in their area—that is, for their defensive actions.

The statistics in table 12.1 illustrate how often some skills come into play during a senior game. Keep in mind that these numbers will vary from team to team depending on such factors as team strategies, game plans, playing

and coaching styles, the success of the team and playing conditions. Also, some defensive skills—chases, bumps, spoils—are not easily quantified, and statistics alone do not show the complete picture. For example, how many kicks and handballs found their mark, or how many opposition disposal errors were brought about by a desperate chase? The statistics do not include this important information.

Table 12.1   Average AFL Statistics per Team per Game (2004)

Offensive skills		Defensive skills	
Kicks	198	Tackles	45
Handballs	118	Shepherds	18
Marks	81	Smothers	6
Points scored	99		

AFL Media Guide, 2005.

Recent statistical analysis of games at the elite level is showing a greater emphasis on offence. An example of this has been the trend to record hard ball gets—the ability of a player to gain possession of a disputed ball on the ground. Players now run much farther during a game than they once did. GPS technology has enabled us to record the offensive demands on the players and the physical requirements needed to meet these demands. Some players at the elite level travel in excess of 20 kilometres a match. That is, they are doing a half marathon while gathering and disposing of the ball, creating offensive opportunities for themselves and teammates as well as undertaking their required defensive responsibilities.

Today's players are faster than those of the past, and so is the movement of the ball. The number of handballs per game has increased fourfold from a few decades back, and there is more emphasis on playing on from marks and free kicks. Fitness tests on players indicate that significantly greater levels of speed and endurance are required for the running, attacking game now played. Players also have to be able to recover more quickly because the modern game of attack gives them less chance to recover after an effort.

The once rare sight of a half back, full back or back-pocket player kicking at goals is much more common in today's fast-flowing, attacking brand of football. The open, running game demanded by today's coaches has replaced the kick-and-mark style and shows the need for players to think offence and to practise offensive skills.

Offence, then, is the name of the modern game. If you don't score, you can't win. Attacking the ball, taking possession of it and then disposing of it to advantage is what the game is all about. Attack the ball and take possession—these are fundamental to offensive football. Don't think of *gaining* possession but of *taking* possession. Be positive. The player with the confident—even arrogant—approach to the ball is hard to beat both in attack and defence.

The legendary AFL coach Allan Jeans once stated, 'If your opponents are held scoreless, your team only has to score one point to win—defence *is* important!' Holding a team scoreless is unlikely, but the point is that all players, no matter what their position, must recognise the crucial role of defence.

Defensive skills and strategies are also fundamental to all game plans. Obviously, some players have greater defensive responsibilities than others do. Players in this category are the six players forming the half-back and full-back lines, the *backmen*. They take intense pride in restricting their opponents to as few possessions as possible and minimising their scoring. Their aggression, confidence, attack on the ball and runs are instrumental to mounting counterattacks, often leading to a goal.

Similarly, players whose position on the field may be in attack will have to be prepared to employ defence against a possible counterattack by the opposition. No player is only an attacker or a defender; games are lost by players forgetting the defensive aspect of the game. The centre line player who does not come out of attack as quickly as he went in, the forward who does not chase, the on-baller/midfield player who does not check, the missed or weak tackle, the lack of discipline to spoil an opponent's mark—these are just a few examples of defensive mistakes that prove costly. Opposition forwards or midfielders known to have a poor defensive side of their game can be exploited by running off them and mounting a counterattack.

Then there is what is often referred to as the *engine room*. These are the midfielders who link the back lines with the forwards. Because they are in the midfield, they tend to be in the play more often. Football commentators are often heard to say that 'the game will be won or lost in the midfield'. However, as we have seen by examples in the preceding steps, a game can be won or lost anywhere on the field. It is how the team performs as a unit that wins or loses games.

Many Australian footballers have developed good technique in the basic facets of the game. They take the ball cleanly, kick long and accurately and bump and tackle well. These players may also possess the agility, quickness, strength and endurance that the game requires. But good technique and skills alone have not enabled these players to become good or even average footballers.

Australian football, like many other sports, requires its players to have the ability to use their skills in game situations. They need to know which actions are appropriate under changing circumstances, how to allow for different environmental conditions, how to counter different opponents, how to perform automatically under game pressure, how to read the play and be in the right place at the right time and how to make things easier for their teammates. That is, the good footballer needs to know the game and possess game skills.

A good player must understand that he cannot practise and perform in isolation and that he needs to learn more than just the skills of handballing, kicking, tackling and so on. Furthermore, he must recognise and understand the requirements of the game and the basic strategies and tactics that lead to success.

Once players have achieved a certain level of skill, their coaches will spend much of practice time employing these skills in team-oriented drills to develop patterns of play. There are many examples of these in this book. These patterns will not only make the skills of the game automatic for a player but will also help him quickly decide what course of action to take in the variety of situations he is likely to confront in a game. Decision making is now seen as fundamental to being an effective player, along with

peripheral vision and reaction time. Again, drills can be devised to develop these aspects.

So this step concerns some of the basic components of game flow—what a team is trying to achieve in a game and how it goes about it. This will include looking at the different positions on the ground and their particular requirements and going over some team patterns and strategies.

Team play is more than tactics, strategies and rules. It is an old but true saying that a good team will usually beat a group of talented individuals. So, we'll also discuss the qualities a good team man possesses, our objective being to make you a more effective player overall.

Teams do not win games merely by getting possession of the ball. Nor does the team with the most scoring shots necessarily win. Teams must make effective use of the ball once they gain it. A team may have more marks, kicks and handballs than its opponent yet still be beaten because its tactics and skills have not put those possessions and disposals to advantage.

FIELD POSITIONS

Manuals on football play and coaching often show maps of ovals with areas shaded to designate coverage by particular players (figure 12.1). Australian football has evolved to the stage at which these positional concepts are no longer relevant for the senior levels. For youngsters these maps are still an appropriate tool to help them understand team play and to prevent them from all following the ball around the field trying to get a kick.

Today's game demands flexibility in roles that include covering a zone, filling a space, blocking a team's strength, roaming the whole field, making rapid use of interchange players, playing man-on-man, maximising particular strengths and many more. For example, whereas a wingman not too long ago knew almost precisely where to play, today's wingman can be expected to cover the whole ground from full forward to full back and on both sides of the ground, depending on team plans and strategies. It is not unusual to see all four wingmen on one side of the oval, a half forward starting behind the

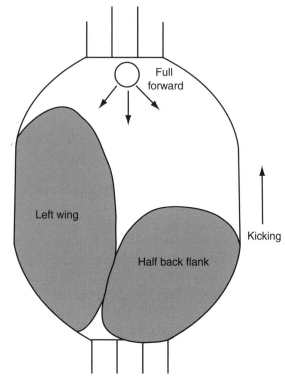

Figure 12.1 Traditional map of players' positions on the field.

centre square and a forward pocket stationed on the wing. The lack of any semblance of a formal offside rule makes this possible. Midfielders or on-ballers at the senior level freely interchange positions and indeed the interchange bench as they go through rotations to recover from exertion or merely to confuse the opposition. This is not nearly so evident or prevalent in junior or amateur football. Teams are still named in position, not only from match to match but also within a single game. Nevertheless, it is still helpful for all players to identify in general terms their possible roles when named in a position. Figure 12.2 shows the names and positions of the 18 players.

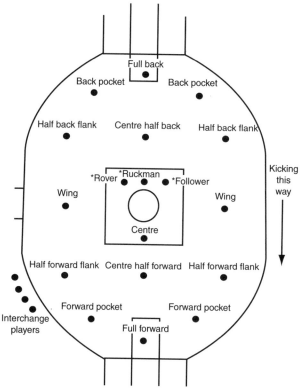

Figure 12.2 Players' positions.

Full-Back Line

The full back and the two back pockets make up the full-back line. These players' fundamental role is to prevent opponents from gaining possession of the ball and kicking goals. They also try to keep their opponents from using the attacking zone in front of the goals.

A full back's performance is ultimately judged by how many goals the opposing full forward kicks. The backs try to spoil their opponents'

attempts to mark, and they defend to deny possession of the ball to the forwards. If the defensive players have the ball, they become running attacking players, moving the ball out of defence into attack.

The back pockets, while being responsible for restricting possession of the ball by their immediate opponents, assist the full back in denying space and the ball to the full forward, who is the likely focal point for opposition attacks.

Half-Back Line

The two half-back flanks and the centre half back are the line of first defence, but they also are an important group for taking possession of the ball and mounting an attack. A successful team has a half-back unit that is dependable on defence but can also carry the ball forward in attack and often kick goals. Effective half-back players are always prepared to run past centre and half-forward teammates to receive a handball or to offer support. They then get back quickly to their immediate opponents and defend.

Centre Line

The centre line includes the two wingmen and the centre player. These three are usually good ball-getting, running players who will help turn defence into attack and set up attacking plays. Their main role is to get the ball to forward players, so they are sometimes called *link men*. These positions are usually manned by very skilled players able to handball with either hand and kick with either foot. They will have good turning agility, an above-average ability to read the play, a high level of fitness and exceptional team skills.

A basic but essential team discipline is that when your opponents have the ball, you defend, and when your team has the ball, you attack. This is especially important for centre line players, who constantly change from attacking to defending and back again. When their team has possession of the ball, the centre line players run to position themselves to receive and relay the ball. Conversely, once the ball has been turned over to their opponents, the centre line players' first objective is to find and defend strongly against their direct opponents.

Because they will run past half-forward players to receive a handball or take the ball off hands and have a shot at goal, centre line players often kick goals. In senior football, as centre line players run towards or beyond the 50-metre line, they will have a shot at goal. Outside that range they tend to pass the ball to full-forward players.

On kickoffs by the opposition, centre line players tend to play behind the players contesting for the mark to be in position to play either a defensive or attacking role depending on which team takes possession of the ball or to chase the ball if it runs loose over the back of the pack.

Half-Forward Line

The half-forward line is made up of the centre half forward and the two half-forward flankers. The centre half forward is usually a tall player who becomes the focal point for attacks out of the back line as the ball is brought into the attacking zone. Therefore, the centre half forward should be able to mark well overhead.

The flankers are generally quick players able to take the ball falling from contested marks and kick accurately for goal on the run. These positions are considered difficult to play; not only are they strongly defended but they also require the player to take the ball and then turn towards his goal unlike other positions that attack the ball straight on and keep going in that direction. Half forwards should work together and not contest marks against each other.

Strong defence is required by half forwards to prevent their opponents from getting the ball and initiating attacking moves. That is, half forwards need to be able to chase and to tackle hard.

Full-Forward Line

The full forward and the two forward-pocket players make up the full-forward line. These are the main goal-scoring players. The full forward is generally a fast leading player to whom teammates will try to kick the ball so that it can be marked and followed by a shot at goal. However, as the ball is often delivered to the area under pressure (and therefore not always accurately), the full forward is also expected to take hotly contested marks and to gather the ball from the ground under pressure. A high-marking full forward who can't or won't contest strongly on the ground will be of limited use to his team.

Usually one pocket player is tall and the other is small. The tall pocket player moves behind the full forward when he leads and becomes a second target for the attacking team. This player should be able to mark well overhead and kick accurately for goal. The small pocket player's major role is to position himself to gather the ball falling from the marking contests of the larger forwards and their opponents. Once he has gathered it, he shoots for goal. This player must have speed, agility, good ball and goal sense and accurate goal shooting.

As with the half forwards, the full-forward line has a vital role in preventing opponents from mounting an attacking move from deep in the forward line. As soon as the opposition has the ball, the forwards must become desperate, ruthless defenders and fight to hold the ball in their area. A forward who will not chase is a liability to his team.

Ruckman

As the largest player on the team, the ruckman has both attacking and defensive roles, particularly when the ball is in the air. He is a focal point for many attacking kicks out of defence but will also position himself to try to intercept kicks by the opposition. Both of these roles come into play when the ball is kicked off following a behind being scored.

To succeed, the ruckman needs to read the play very well. One of his fundamental roles is to position himself near the opposing team's centre half forward to contest marks and in front of the full forward to deny him space into which to lead. He should also be in position to contest marks with the full forward and the larger of the forward pockets.

Ruck Rover and Rover

The ruck rover and the rover, sometimes referred to as *on-ballers*, roam the field and initiate many attacking moves. They cover opponents' attacking players, provide additional coverage all over the field and are important links in establishing attacking moves.

These players will have exceptional ball-getting and disposal skills. They will be able to read the play and get to where the ball is. Their play is characterized by fearless winning of the ball, tackling and a willingness to run for the entire game. Although primarily attacking players, they defend well, covering their counterparts when the opposition has the ball.

Sometimes a ruck rover or a rover is given a more defensive role. That is, he becomes a *run-with player*. This means that a coach has identified one of the opposition players as a particularly dangerous threat and designates one of his on-ballers to cover that player wherever he goes. Although this role is primarily a defensive one, it does not mean that the defensive player sacrifices his game completely. He will still try to get the ball and create attacking opportunities for himself as well and will have the advantage in that his opponent will be taking him to the ball in the first place.

Interchange Players

Each team is allowed to start four interchange players, although this may vary with the level being played. These are versatile players who play a variety of positions. Players are freely interchangeable during the game as long as the interchanges occur at the designated part of the field and the interchange official is notified.

Interchange players used to feel that they were merely reserve players who sat on the bench because they weren't quite good enough to make the team. This is not the case in today's game. These players, certainly at the elite level, are integral and important members of the team structure. Teams will give considerable thought to which players fill this role depending on weather conditions and specific strategies.

GAME PLAN STRATEGIES

Australian football is very much a player-on-player game. Although the concept of zones is apparent in game tactics, these are not so much zones for players (because now some players are encouraged to roam much of the field), but zones of play.

Figure 12.3 shows the scoring (attacking) defensive zones. In kicking for goal, the optimal position is from directly in front, so a team wishing to maximise its offensive efforts attempts to get the ball into this position as often as possible. Conversely, the defensive team works to keep the ball out of this area. These two simplistic statements are a generalization of the main strategies of Australian football; all more sophisticated tactics are built on that foundation.

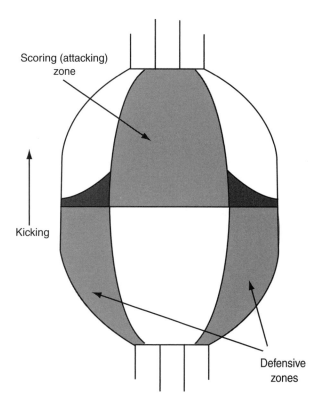

Figure 12.3 Zones of play.

In general terms, then, a team's basic game plan is to get the ball into its scoring zone and shoot for goal and to deny the opposition from so doing by keeping it to the defensive flanks.

Defence

Apart from trying to gain possession of the ball, the fundamental aim of the defence is to force the opponent into a position that minimises the effectiveness of its possession.

When kicking out from a point or in general play, back players will rarely kick straight down the field from deep in defence. Instead they will

131

kick to players who have led from the opponent's scoring zone into the defensive flanks.

Rather than turning back and kicking into the middle of the field, players in the back lines will try to turn so that the kick goes to the defensive zone. When contesting a loose ball in the back lines, back players should try to force the ball towards the boundary and not back into play.

At boundary throw-ins, the ruckman should attempt to bring the ball to the ground forward of the pack close to the boundary line. He should never try to hit the ball back over his head into the opponent's scoring zone.

Kicking across goals is risky. However, it can be an effective way to establish an attack by switching the attack's direction. This is generally done deep in defence, where the ball is driven wide to the opposite defensive zone. Doing this, players need to kick the ball long so that the receiver does not have to come back to meet the ball and so an inaccurate kick runs towards the boundary line, away from the opponent's attacking zone.

Defensive players position themselves between their opponents and the goal to force attackers to turn towards the defensive flank and away from the team's scoring zone. This position also forces the attacking player to lead to the outside.

When pursuing an attacking player, the defender should try to chase from the inside and force the attacker towards the boundary (figure 12.4). This prevents easy access to the scoring zone.

A defensive player should determine which side his opponent prefers for disposal and anticipate moves to that side. Forcing an opponent onto his wrong leg and away from the scoring zone is effective defence.

Ruckmen will try to move back into the free space in front of the opposing key forwards in the scoring zone. This reduces the options available for the forwards to lead and forces them to move into the defensive flanks. This positioning also causes those delivering the ball to kick it high, thus making it easier to spoil.

When a forward has possession in the defensive zones, defenders should anticipate a kick to the scoring zone. This is particularly important in situations in which the attackers have a free

kick or a mark in this area. They may kick the ball backwards to gain a better position. Good defence will force the player to kick for goal from his poor position.

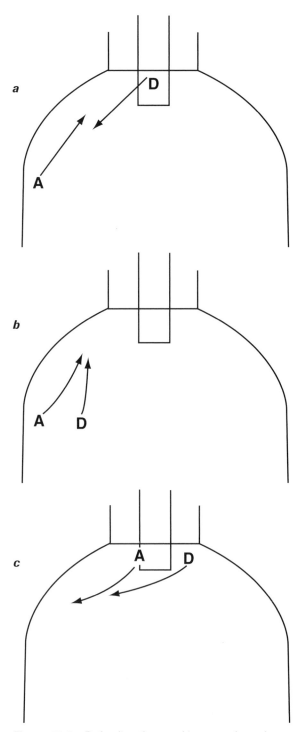

Figure 12.4 Defending the attacking zone. In each case the defender (D) moves to a position in which the only direction available for the attacker is towards the boundary line and away from the attacking zone (corridor).

Attack

In attack, players usually position themselves so that their preferred foot will naturally kick the ball into the attacking zone when making a turn. Attackers usually start from the defensive zones of the opposition, and their leads take them into the scoring zone. To create space in the attacking area, the half forwards often play up the field and lead back towards goal.

On taking possession, a player should attempt to turn so that his kick will go into the scoring zone.

The ball should be centred whenever possible. From the flanks the ball should be kicked to the head of the kickoff square.

Space can be created in the attacking zone by leading out to the flank and then doubling back. This can be done by one player making a dummy lead out of the scoring zone and another player leading into the space created.

It is important not to crowd the scoring zone. Centre line players should not go into this area too soon. It is better to go in at the same time as the ball and read it off hands or take the handball at top speed.

The ball should be moved forwards into the attacking area quickly before defensive ruckmen and centre players can crowd the scoring space.

Players all over the ground will try to create space to initiate an attacking move. That is, players will make space by running, leaving space behind them that other players might run into and have the ball kicked to them.

Coming out of defence, players should not centre the ball too early. An interception will give the opponent good attacking position.

The ruckman will try to knock some of the boundary throw-ins back into the scoring zone. At other times he will try to get the ball to players moving into the scoring zone.

Forward players should anticipate their defensive opponents' trying to clear the ball to the flanks. They should try to block this movement and force them to kick the ball to the middle of the field.

Good defensive players read the ball well and anticipate what the attackers are trying to do. Therefore, this needs to be countered by quick running movements and short kicks over the defensive players or line.

Ruckwork

The game is started at each quarter and restarted after each goal by a bounce in the centre circle. Only four players from each team may be in the square until the ball touches the ground. This controlled situation allows for set plays to be used in taking the ball out of the square. There are many such plays, but they are based on three strategies.

For *man-on-man* play, a team decides that it will simply man up on opponents in the square (figure 12.5). A team usually uses this tactic if it has good ball getters in the square or as a defensive move if the other team is getting the ball out of the square too often.

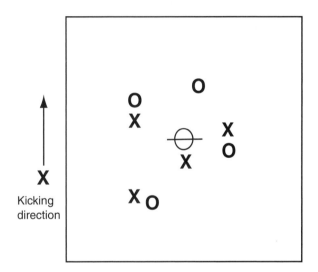

Figure 12.5 Man-on-man positioning.

In *zoned placement,* each of the four players controls a specific area (figure 12.6). Usually the follower positions on the defensive side of the circle towards the back of the square to cover the ball coming out. The rover is placed on the ruckman's arm—that is, where the ruckman expects to put the ball. The centre player is usually on the attacking side of the circle to assist the rover or to defend if the opponents take possession in this area.

For *check side placement,* a team concedes that the opposition ruckman is likely to win

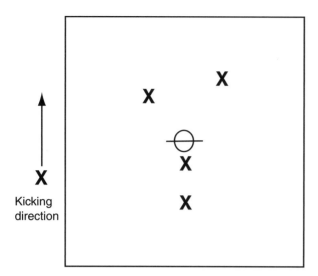

Figure 12.6   Zoned placement positioning.

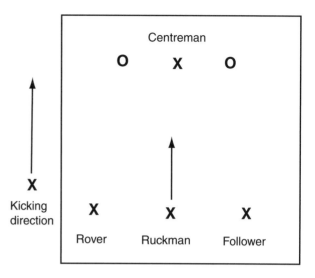

Figure 12.8   Common ball up positioning.

the knock and place it in a particular area. The team places players in that area, and their own ruckman also tries to get the ball to that position (figure 12.7).

A common combination of these tactics is to place the rover on the ruckman's arm, the follower covering the zone on the defensive side of the circle and the centreman going man on man on the opposition rover (figure 12.8).

When there is a ball up following a scrimmage, the tactics are not as clear-cut because more players are about the ball and the bounce can be at any position on the field. Generally, in this situation a check side is used. The tactic is that the follower and rover position themselves

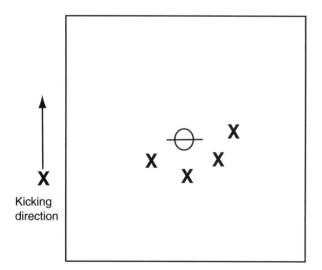

Figure 12.7   Check side positioning.

between the bounce and their opponent's goal. The ruckman attempts to bring the ball back, giving them possession as they move straight towards their own goal. If the opposition gets the knock, the rover and follower are already moving towards them for a tackle or smother, which will force the opponents to run wide to attack. A position player will need to be stationed within the opposition to try to prevent them from taking possession.

An adaptation of this tactic is used for boundary throw-ins, in which the ruckman attempts to put the ball down to the check (defensive) side so that when the ball is taken, the players' movement is in the direction of the goals. The ensuing movement depends on whether the throw-in is in attack or defence. In defence, the players try to keep the ball close to the boundary by the ruckman knocking forwards (figure 12.9a). In attack, he will attempt to hit to the side or the back so that once the ball is gathered it can be taken inside to a better scoring position (figure 12.9b). In all cases it is vital to have at least one position player stationed among the opposition to defend and another to cover the back of the pack to defend the hit there.

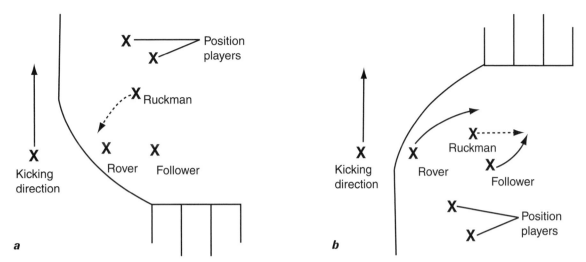

Figure 12.9 Boundary throw-in tactics: *(a)* in defence, *(b)* in attack.

KICKOFFS

The only other time during the game that set plays can be planned is when the ball is kicked out after a behind has been scored. Here there are several options.

Any player can kick off. (It has already been established that the ball is usually kicked wide to the defensive flanks out of the opponent's scoring zone.) The long kick is directed to the leading player moving from the midline of the field to the flank. If the team has a strong mark, it is usual to play towards him. The opposition will try to counter this, so another option needs to be available. If the opposition has a dominant marking player, it is of course good sense to kick it away from him.

The short kick to a player—usually a winger, back pocket or half back who leads to the pocket—is a good way of establishing an attacking play by creating a loose man, particularly if the alert player runs past the receiver, takes the ball back and then kicks it long. The short kickoff does come at a cost though. In kicking short to a pocket, the kicking team retains the ball, but staying close to goal and going to the pocket effectively cuts out half the ground that the opposition team has to protect. Because of this, teams often concede a short kickoff to a player deep in the pocket. In this case both the attacking and defending teams have to plan for the second kick.

Figure 12.10 illustrates the concept of making space for a kickoff, which is an important team tactic. Teams may group together and prior to kickoff scatter into spaces where the ball will

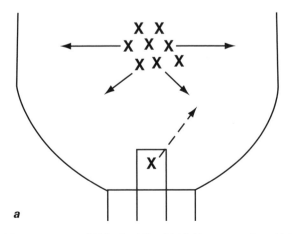

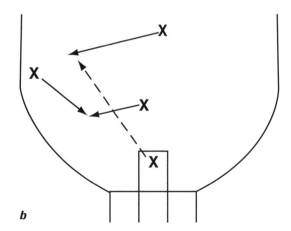

Figure 12.10 *(a)* The huddle. *(b)* Making space for a kickoff.

be kicked. A variation of this is to designate a player to make a dummy lead to create space into which the ball will be kicked as another player moves into that space.

The player kicking the football back into play may, provided he has kicked the football clear from his hands, regain possession and play on from within the goal square. Because the full forward must be back from the head of the goal square, the player kicking off has an advantage (particularly if this tactic is employed close to the goal line) and can run the ball out of the area to create the loose man or to kick the ball over the waiting pack to a player running into attack.

If in doubt as to where to kick the ball, or if there is a following wind, the player kicking off will probably kick the ball as far as possible to the defensive zones or straight down the middle to get as close as possible to his team's attacking zone.

Defence of the kickoff is either man-on-man or, if the opposition is grouping, cover zones (figure 12.11).

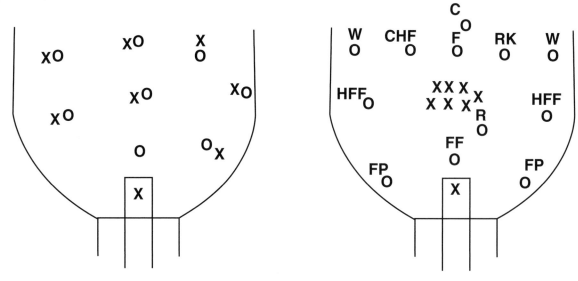

Figure 12.11 Defence of the kickoff: *(a)* man-on-man; *(b)* zone. The most common zone pattern is lines of three, four and five players.

GAME CONDITIONS

A good team adapts its game plan and tactics to the weather. Adverse conditions will affect both teams, and the team best able to adapt will have an advantage. The element that affects the game most is the wind, as the flight of the ball is noticeably affected.

A following wind carries a kick a greater distance, making it imperative that there are players on the ground behind the pack to take the falling ball off hands. Kicking with the wind is an advantage that players need to capitalise on. Generally the ball is kicked long, straight and quickly. A mistake can be in taking the wind for granted. Even with wind, kicks need to be directed to players and spaces; the main difference is that with a following wind the kicker can look farther afield for his target.

When defending against the wind, it is best to slow the game down and keep the ball wide on the ground. Attacking against the wind, though difficult, often results in good team football because the game becomes one of running, sharing and possession. The ball is carried into the wind by low trajectory kicks and handpasses combined with running the ball using several teammates.

A crosswind often results in low-scoring, tight games. In these conditions players should consider the zones to have been moved across the field towards the wind, as shown in figure 12.12. That is, players defend to the leeward side of the ground and attack from the windward side.

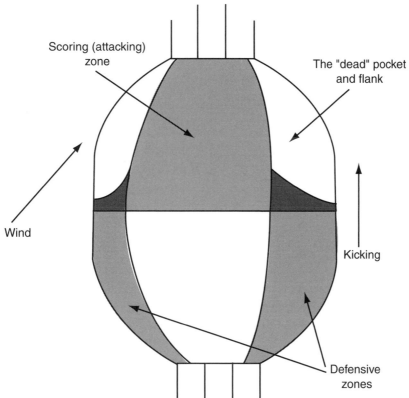

Figure 12.12 Playing in windy conditions.

PLAY READING

Because basic tactics form most game plans, they are used by both teams. Hence a team often suspects what an opponent will do in a given situation. Of course the opposition is aware of these suspicions and will sometimes alter its tactics in an attempt to catch the other team by surprise. Here is where the glorious uncertainty of sport takes over and where superior skill (and some luck) influences the result.

An important skill in most sports, including Australian football, is the ability to read a play. This skill involves understanding the basic tactics of the game, incorporating knowledge of teammates' and opponents' strengths and weaknesses and responding to information coming in regarding the flight of the ball, the weather, the condition of the ground, the positions of other players, the type of kick used and the like. Processing all this information enables the player to anticipate where the ball is going, perhaps even while it is still a kick or two away. This skill varies from player to player, but all players can improve through practice, attention to detail and, above all, concentration.

TEAM PLAY

Team play is more than tactics and strategies. Good teams are made up of individuals who endeavour to play their part in advantaging their teammates and disadvantaging the opposition. All players can contribute to their team's success in the way they approach the game and by following guidelines established by the team and the coach. The good team player possesses a variety of qualities.

- He is committed, confident and disciplined.
- He goes to meet the ball and does not wait for it to come to him. His approach on the

ball is straight and aggressive. His approach on the player is equally straight and hard but is also legal. A player who gives away needless free kicks is not a good team player.

- He talks to his teammates. Not every player will be outgoing, but a team player needs to let his teammates know what is going on around them as they go for the ball. Talk should always be positive and encouraging.

- He knows his own strengths and weaknesses as well as those of teammates and the opposition.

- He recovers his position after a play so that an intercepted ball is not easily sent back to his uncontested opponent.

- He moves back quickly to take his kick from a mark or free kick and does not turn his back on the play. This enables him to look for options to kick, handball or play on.

- He will man up on his opponent whenever his opponent has the ball.

- He recovers quickly after falling. A player on the ground is a noncontributing player.

- He won't allow a teammate going for the ball to be outnumbered. He positions to back him up, talks to him and protects him by shepherding.

- He kicks long to position or to the moving player and kicks short only when possession to a teammate is virtually assured.

- He doesn't consider his job done once he has disposed of the ball. He runs past to be in a position to receive the ball back if necessary, backs up his teammates in case of a fumble, blocks and shepherds his teammates to allow them to dispose without pressure and then gets back to his position to cover his opponent.

- He takes front position over the ball. This is where he will get the free kicks.

- He gets down to the ball in packs and knocks it out to teammates, through for a point or to the boundary.

- He chases an opponent when there is little or no chance of catching him but when the chase may cause a fumble or a ball-handling error.

- He spoils and doesn't attempt to mark when out of position.

- He doesn't allow a ruckman, follower or rover to stand a mark or free kick.

Many drills have been developed to practise team plays. These drills exemplify the team discipline that coaches demand of their players. Generally, the drills cannot be done alone or even in small groups; they are usually kept until formal practice. However, what follows are a few drills you can try if you have five or six friends who want to improve basic team patterns to make themselves better team players. Generally, the object of the drills is to provide many opportunities to practise concepts of team play, team disciplines and movement patterns. For each of the drills, make the distances between players and the size of the field appropriate to the size and skill of the players practising.

Team Drill 1. *Head of the Square*

Remember that the object of good forward team play is to get the ball into the best possible scoring position, usually directly in front of the goals. Player A rolls the ball in the direction of and close to the boundary (figure 12.13). Player B runs after the ball, picks it up and, instead of trying to kick the goal from an almost impossible angle, kicks it high to the head of the square for player C to mark. Change positions after each kick; have 10 kicks each.

To Increase Difficulty

- Try the drill again from the other side of the goals. Because you will probably be practising with your nondominant foot, try to have your kicks marked in the goal square at least 8 times out of 10.

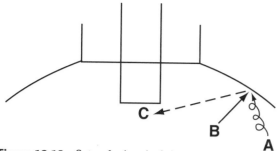

Figure 12.13 Setup for head-of-the-square drill.

Success Check

- Kick the ball with some height but not so high that in a game it could be easily spoiled.
- Turn your body so that you are square on to your target.
- Don't kick around corners.

Team Drill 2. *Handball Option*

If a player is facing the opposite direction to which his team is attacking, he shouldn't have to turn and kick upon receiving the ball. It is good team play for teammates to run past him for the handball.

a

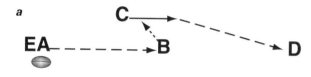

b

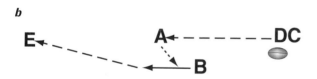

Figure 12.14 Setup for handball-option drill.

Try this drill in a group of five. Player A kicks the ball to player B, who marks it as player C runs past (figure 12.14a). Player C calls for the handball and then kicks to player D. Player D now kicks the ball to player A, who has taken player C's position (figure 12.14b). Player B runs past player A, gets the handball and kicks to player E. The process starts again as the drill continues.

Success Check

- Time your run to take the ball at speed.
- Time your run so that you take the ball in front.
- When handballing, do so with the correct hand.
- Do not make it an effort for the receiving player.

Team Drill 3. *Defend and Score*

When kicking away from goal, a defender usually tries to go close to the boundary line. Attackers try to get the ball towards the midline of the ground to score. In this drill player A, defending, kicks the ball to player B, who is close to the boundary line (figure 12.15). Player B passes to player C, who has run from near the centre to take the ball and run straight at goal to try a shot. Player C follows the ball and takes player A's place, player A takes player B's place, and player B takes player C's place. Here it is important for player A to get the ball close to the boundary and player B to get his pass in front of player C so player C can kick the goal.

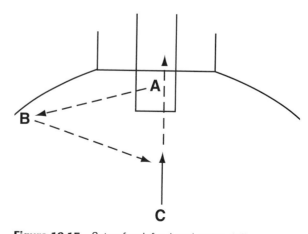

Figure 12.15 Setup for defend-and-score drill.

Success Check

- Make all your kicks accurate.

- Pass the ball in front of player C, who should not have to slow down or break stride.
- Kick the goal.

Team Drill 4. *Cover the Turnover*

Sometimes a player takes a risk and leaves his opponent to attack. However, if the ball is intercepted, the good team player will make every endeavour to get back to cover his opponent.

Player A kicks the ball to player B (who marks it) and races after it to receive a handball back from player B (figure 12.16a). He then kicks the ball to player D, who plays the part of the intercepting player. Player A then has to turn and sprint back to his starting point before player D kicks the ball to player B, runs past for the handball from player B and kicks to player E (figure 12.16b). In other words, player A has to beat the ball back to player E. Player E now becomes the intercepting player and has to get the ball to player B and beat player D back to his starting point.

Success Check

- Keep your kicks low and accurate.

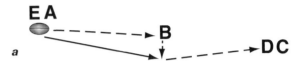
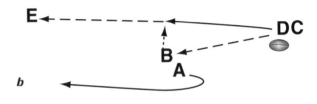

Figure 12.16 Setup for cover-the-turnover drill.

- Do this at top pace.
- Turn sharply once you have kicked to the end players.
- Beat the ball back to your starting point.

Team Drill 5. *Tap It On*

It is often impossible to take the ball and handball to a teammate. In such cases it is good play to knock the ball out in front of him so that he can pick it up under less pressure. Player C rolls the ball between player A and player B but closer to player A than to player B (figure 12.17). Player A gets to the ball first and knocks it back to player C, who is able to pick it up. Continually rotate positions and the direction of the roll.

Success Check

- Bend your knees to get down to the ball.
- Hold your position against the opposing player.
- Knock the ball out accurately to your teammate.
- Do not scoop the ball, which would be penalised for a throw.

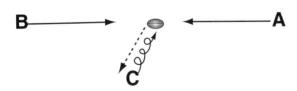

Figure 12.17 Setup for tap-it-on drill.

Team Drill 6. *Give and Go*

Too often players handball or kick the ball and think that their job is done. This drill requires the player who has given the handball to chase after it and try to execute a tackle. Players are in groups of five. Player A handballs to player B, who handballs to player C, who handballs to player D, who handballs to player E (figure 12.18). All players are running forwards to the markers except for player A, who runs behind the group trying to get close enough to player E to tackle him before he reaches the marker. Change positions after each

run with each player having several turns at being the chaser and the chased.

Success Check

- All players move at top speed and apart from the chaser, in a straight line.
- Handball accurately in front of the running players so they can take the ball at speed.
- Make sure all tackles are legal.

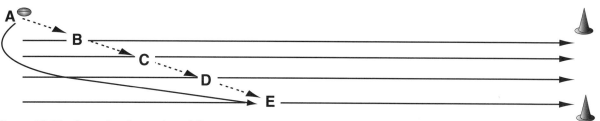

Figure 12.18 Setup for give-and-go drill.

Team Drill 7. *Run Inside*

On a diagram of a football field, the attacking zone is in the middle. In actual play there is often space to the outside, and players run here to the disadvantage of their team. Players should get into the habit early of running inside.

In this drill, player A kicks to player B, who marks and handballs to player C, who has run inside to take the ball and kick the goal (figure 12.19). To get the ball back to the starting position, player D kicks to player E on the boundary line and player E runs up to take the place of player A. In the meanwhile, player A becomes player B, B becomes C, C becomes D and D becomes E.

Success Check

- Time your run to take the ball at speed.
- Kick the ball low and accurately to the player in the goal square.

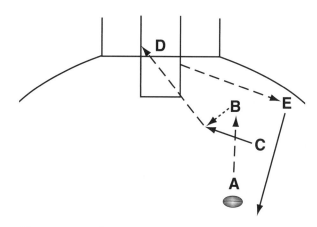

Figure 12.19 Setup for run-inside drill.

- In kicking to the player near the boundary, try to get close to the boundary but not out on the full.

Team Drill 8. *Kick, Mark, Handball*

A potent part of attacking team play is to handball forwards to a running player, often enabling the next kick to clear defenders who have set themselves to intercept.

In this drill, player A kicks high to player B, who marks and handballs to either player C or player D as they run forwards (figure 12.20). The receiving player then kicks to the middle person of the next group, and the process is repeated. After each mark and handball, all three players involved run to the other end of the drill.

Figure 12.20   Setup for kick, mark, handball drill.

Success Check

- Time your run so that you are not too far in advance of the handballing player and have to turn to take the ball.

- The handballing player must handball the ball in front of the running players. If they have to stop or slow, the handballer would have been better off kicking the ball himself.
- As they are coming from behind, the receiving players should call for the ball early from the midperson.

Team Drill 9. *Kickoff*

Have one player play the part of the full back kicking off. Other players huddle together until the full back is ready to kick off. As the full back prepares to kick off, all other players sprint in various directions to give many targets for the kickoff (figure 12.21). The full back tries to get the ball on the full or in front of one of the running players. Change kickoff player regularly (after five kicks or so).

Success Check

- Huddle players sprint away from the group.
- The kickoff player varies his kicks—some short, some to the side and some long.

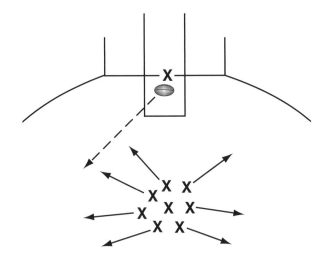

Figure 12.21   Setup for kickoff drill.

Team Drill 10. *Six Stations*

Six players practise defensive and offensive use of the football field. Player A kicks the ball to player B, who is leading towards the defensive edge of

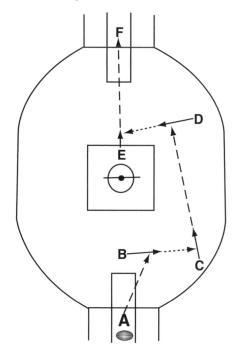

Figure 12.22 Setup for six-stations drill.

the field (figure 12.22). Player C runs past for a handball and kicks the ball down the side of the field to player D, who is leading into the attacking corridor. Player D handballs to player E, who is running straight at goal and has a shot. Player F recovers the ball and starts the ball back in the other direction with all players taking reverse roles. After the ball goes back to the start, players A, B and C change positions, as do players D, E and F. Don't use all of the football ground; it is too long. Put in your own markers to act as goals so that players can reach them without too much running and bouncing between stations.

Success Check

- This drill has most kicks to a player leading at an angle to the kicker. Therefore, it is important to kick the ball in front of the leading player.

- The kicks should be given some height and at a speed that allows the leading player to make some adjustment to take the ball if necessary.

Team Drill 11. *Goal Race*

Divide your group into two teams, each with its own ball. On a signal, the two teams kick the ball off from the kickoff square and try to be the first to score a goal at the other end of the field (figure 12.23). Score 1 point for being first to score. When taking the ball down the ground, each team must stay on its side of the ground and not go into the centre square. After each goal and when both teams are ready, another signal is given and the race is repeated in the opposite direction. The first team to score 5 points wins.

Success Check

- Move the ball on quickly and accurately.
- Take the ball while moving.

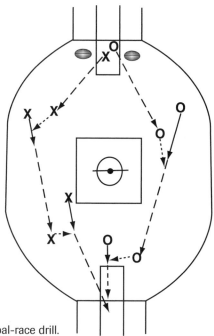

Figure 12.23 Setup for goal-race drill.

Team Drill 12. *Shadowing*

The concept of shadowing—running with another player—can be applied to many of the team drills to add some pressure or just to give a player experience and practice in staying close to an opponent.

Players partner up for simple lane work but with a player applying pressure by just shadowing and staying as close as possible. No contact is allowed. Player A has the ball and runs forwards, closely followed by player C. Player B leads, closely followed by player D. Player A passes the ball to player B, who is pressured but not spoiled or intercepted by player D. Players A and C run through and get on the line and change roles next turn.

This drill can be varied to be made more difficult and to promote the concept of following the kick. Player A, shadowed by player C, passes to player B, who is shadowed but not spoiled or intercepted by player D. Players A and C follow the pass to receive the handball from player B (figure 12.24). Players B and D run through to the other line. The ball is then handballed to either player E or player F. The one not receiving the handball becomes the player to apply pressure. The ball is kicked down to player G, who is leading with pressure from player H. Players run through each time and change roles next turn.

Success Check

- Stay in contact with the player you are shadowing.

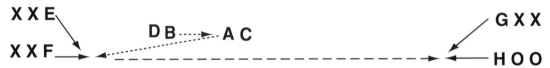

Figure 12.24 More difficult variation of shadowing drill.

Team Drill 13. *Switch of Play*

More advanced team drills require an ability to kick the ball long and therefore are more appropriate for senior players. These drills can be done with younger players by using markers to reduce the size of the playing field.

For advanced players, set up a square 50 metres by 30 metres. Player A starts with the ball at one corner. He kicks long to player B, who marks, turns and kicks (switches) the ball to player C using a low, flat kick (figure 12.25). Player C marks and kicks long to player D, who marks and switches the play back to the first group. Players follow their kicks to the next group.

Success Check

- Your kicks are accurate.
- You run to follow up your kicks and back up for any ball-handling errors and spilled balls.

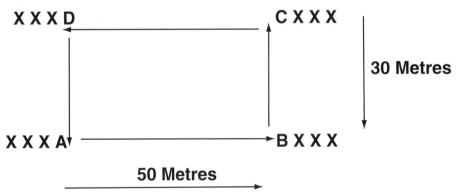

Figure 12.25 Setup of switch-of-play drill.

Team Drill 14. *Look Inside*

This drill is designed to get players to instinctively look for the running player inside the scoring corridor. Player A starts with the ball deep in the back lines. He kicks to player B, who is near the boundary line (figure 12.26). He marks and delivers a kick into the middle wing, player C, near the point of the square. Player C marks and looks inside for player D, who is running past and handballs to him. Player D kicks to player E near centre half forward. Player E marks and handballs to player F back on the inside. Player F kicks to player G, who leads out of the goal square. Player G marks, then kicks the goal.

Success Check

- All kicks and handballs are accurate.
- The ball is moved on quickly at all times.
- The ball is taken on the move.
- Kick the goal.

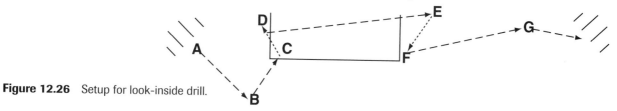

Figure 12.26 Setup for look-inside drill.

Team Drill 15. *Diamond Shape Kicking*

Player A starts with the ball. He handballs to player B, who is running past and who kicks to player C on the wing (figure 12.27). Player C marks and handballs to player D, who is running past and who kicks to player E. Player E handballs to player F, and so on. Each player follows the ball to the next group.

Success Check

- Always handball and kick in front of the player so he can take the ball without breaking stride.
- Time your run to enable the previous player to take the ball and then get it to you in the best position for you to take and dispose.

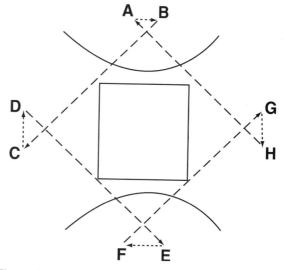

Figure 12.27 Setup for diamond-shape-kicking drill.

TEAM TACTICS AND STRATEGIES SUCCESS SUMMARY

With these team drills it has not been appropriate to have specific scoring and targets for you to achieve. However, what you should do after a team training session when you are filling in your training diary (see next step, training) is go through the drills that you did and give yourself a grade on your overall handballing, marking, kicking and so on. At this time you should also identify areas that need more work. Once you have done that, you can go back over the steps in this book, review the guidelines and do some of the drills, and then at your next training session aim to show an improvement.

Training

The terms *practice* and *training* tend to be used interchangeably, but there is a difference. A player goes to training to practise his own skills as well as team skills and strategies. Practice is the actual doing. But during practice, a player generally has someone—a teacher or a coach, perhaps another player—directing him and his teammates in that process. The skills and drills are organised and directed. Someone else evaluates the player's attempts and offers feedback. This is the training aspect. *Training* means to educate, to teach, to cause to act in a particular way.

A sign in our training facility reads, 'Practice is a rehearsal for performance'. Practice does not make perfect; it makes permanent. Training sessions—how they are organised, what is done at them and how they are used—are a very important part of the player's practising to prepare for *better* performance. Therefore, the coach's and teacher's role is vital in planning, motivating, coordinating, analysing, evaluating, suggesting, changing and challenging so that the player improves his performance of the skill.

There are many facets of skill learning and development, and the player and coach should understand and follow each one, not necessarily in theory but certainly in practice. The first step is to establish a picture or a model in the mind of the performer of what he should do and how he should do it. This is usually achieved by a demonstration or, in the case of some team drills and strategies, by a diagram on the board or walking the players through the planned movements. (Some teams in fact have a diagram of the football field painted on the floor of their training facility to facilitate this.) Part of this process may include an explanation; for example, 'When kicking into the wind, make contact with the ball lower to the ground. This gives the ball a lower trajectory as it is punched into the wind and, as a result, it doesn't float' or 'When standing your opponent, keep him in the side closest to the boundary line. This way, if he gets the ball, he will have to turn in towards you to go towards his goals'.

Explaining why and how to perform a skill differentiates the teacher and the coach from the animal trainer. The lion tamer can train the lion to jump through the hoop, but the lion has no understanding of how it is done or how to adapt the jump in a different situation. Nor does the lion go off and play with the other lions jumping through hoops after the training session! Essentially, however, the detail in both the description and explanation needs to be kept at a level appropriate to the age and experience of the players. Information overload confuses and not infrequently frustrates.

The second step in skill development is to let the player have a try. No one learns a skill just by watching. The player has to try to match what he thinks he should do with an actual attempt. Having tried, he then needs to be told or shown how well he did. There needs to be an evaluation of the performance. Sometimes this is obvious (the beginning player missed the ball in attempting to kick it) and sometimes it is not (the player's handball hit the target but he dropped the ball from his hand as he hit it). Again, the amount of detail in the feedback will depend on the age and experience of the player. The role of the coach is to provide information and advice over many attempts to help the player modify and adapt his performance to match it with the model. Achieving this, the player has developed technique.

The next step in the skill-learning process is to provide opportunities to use the new technique in gamelike and game situations. At this stage the player has to employ the appropriate skill automatically without thinking about it or without focusing on the pressure that may cause the technique to fall apart.

These separate steps to skill development should have been evident throughout this book. The reasons each skill is important are described. Each skill is then explained with specific points to look for. The player attempts the skill, and the coach gives feedback and provides corrections. The player is then allowed to practise the skill under pressure with scored drills and finally incorporates the skill into matchlike situations. The culmination has been to focus on using all the skills of football in team play and the execution of the game plan, which require the player to place his skills on automatic as he reads the play and commits to team tactics and strategy while also concentrating on his opponents.

We have quite deliberately gone through these steps and restated some of what has appeared elsewhere in the book because it is important that players and coaches alike, whatever their level, understand their roles in the development of their skills and becoming better players and coaches.

EFFECTIVE TRAINING

For training to be effective, the player must understand and follow the principles of training, regardless of the sport or the age and experience of the player. All training principles need to be considered in the planning of both long-term programs and individual training sessions. The following principles are the keys to effective training.

1. *Match the training to the players.* Pitch the skills and drills, and indeed expectations, to the players. The younger and more inexperienced the player, the simpler and more basic the activities should be and the shorter the training sessions should be. Fundamentally, with very young and beginning players the emphasis should be on awakening their interest, maintaining their enthusiasm for the activity and teaching them basic skills while making sure they have fun. Training sessions should be short and varied with minimum talk and maximum activity and participation.

The next level, for slightly older and experienced players, incorporates slightly longer training sessions. Older players have longer attention spans and are able to do more physically. At this stage more emphasis can be placed on developing better technique with a greater range of skills and activities. Drills can be a little more complex, but need to be relatively short and varied to maintain interest with some controlled competitive aspects. The adolescent player can cope with increased training loads (in regard to the length of sessions), more demanding drills and increased competition. More can be expected of older players in performing with proper techniques. There may well be a time and opportunity to introduce special training such as some emphasis on fitness and controlled weight training.

Even with adult players the coach needs to be aware of the capabilities of the players. There will be a marked difference in what can be done with and expected of amateur teams who train once a week, state league teams at the semiprofessional level, and the elite performers of the AFL.

2. *Recognise that each player is different.* Coaches need to understand that although they are working with a team, that team is made up of individuals and each one of them will be unique. Even if players are of approximately the same age, they will differ in size, maturity (both physical and social), interests, fitness, abilities, motivation and expectations. The coach will need to do a balancing act between the needs of the team as a whole and the sensitivities and differences of the individuals on the team.

3. *Use the principles of adaptation and overload.* The person as a whole and individual parts of the body adapt to stresses. The same can be said about a team. These adaptations usually occur quite subtly.

Basically, the purpose of training is to increase the demands on the individual players and team so that positive changes occur as they adapt to those demands. These need to be planned for. Practising the same things at the same pace under the same stresses will not create improvement. As the old saying goes, Practice makes permanent; perfect practice makes perfect.

Training needs to incorporate ways to overload the player or the team. This can be done in many ways. In fitness work, the coach might increase the frequency, intensity and time of the activity or reduce recovery time. Introducing targets, providing other options or adding a competitive element are some ways to push players in their skill acquisition. With all training, the coach should be prepared to use varia-

tions to place greater stress. However, the stresses or pressures must not overload to the extent that the player, the team or the skill breaks down. This brings us to the principle of progression.

4. *Use the principle of progression.* Progression is the principle of 'bend but don't break'. Adaptations to training are usually subtle. Therefore, the coach needs to ensure that training overload is not so great that, rather than adapt, the players experience a deterioration in performance.

Progression is also important in the skill-learning process. Progress from the known to the unknown, from the simple to the complex, from the individual to the small group, from the group to the team.

5. *Use the principle of specificity.* Training needs to be specific and, whenever possible, to mirror match requirements. Performance improves most when training is specific to the activity. This is why, when planning a training session, coaches should set specific objectives and choose training drills that address those objectives. If the objective is to improve team tackling, then having drills that include only minimal tackling will make meeting that objective unlikely. If skill training is meant to also improve player fitness (as it should for younger players), having drills that have players standing in line waiting their turn will not achieve any improvement. Australian football involves many short periods of varying durations of high-intensity effort followed by short periods of recovery. Therefore, in training, doing everything at a comfortable pace with long periods of rest between will not do much for match fitness.

6. *Add variation.* A motivated player will train and play with enthusiasm. Boredom demotivates players and lessens their interest. When players are bored, the learning and improvement processes stall and indeed may go backwards. Players become stale. The player who comes to

training knowing that the session is likely to be more of the same old thing is not in the optimum state of mind to maximise the time spent practising.

Variations in content, intensity, challenge, length and perhaps venue of session will lessen players' demotivation and heighten their interest. Maximum involvement, variety, plenty of activity, games, relays and fun are important. We should never forget that Australian football is a game, a great game. It should never become a chore, particularly for young players in whose hands and love for the game its future rests.

PLAYER PREPARATION FOR TRAINING

A number of familiar sayings or mottos could be used here, but the most often used 'As you train, so shall you play' and 'You will get only out what you are prepared to put in' are probably the most appropriate. Training shouldn't be seen as a necessary evil to enable you to play.

Even the professional footballers with whom we work enjoy themselves and generally have fun while working very hard at many training sessions during the week over most of the year. They don't necessarily laugh at much of the hard work, but they enjoy it. For anyone, if training becomes a drag, he will not get the maximum benefit from it.

Come prepared to train. Have some expectation about training and look forward to it with some enthusiasm.

Look the part. You are at football training. Look like a footballer by wearing appropriate clothing and uniform. Have some pride in your football appearance.

Have a plan as to what you want to achieve in the training session. Remember, training is directed practice, and practice is preparation for performance. Identify one thing you particularly want to improve during the session. Give yourself little targets to achieve during particular drills or over the complete practice session.

Listen to the coach's instructions. If in doubt, ask. Concentrate. Be aware that your teammates will also be there to improve so don't distract them while they are trying to listen or waiting to have their turn.

Don't stay in your comfort zone and rely only on those things you do well. When the occasion occurs, use those skills you might not be as confident with. Practise kicking with your preferred kicking leg certainly, but also practise using the other as well. Do the same for handballing.

Don't do everything at half pace. Once you have developed a skill, put it to the test by using it at top speed. In a game, you certainly will have to perform at top speed, and that's not a good place to find out that the skill is more difficult to perform flat out.

Test yourself. In partner work, don't always use the same opponent. Seek out someone who is bigger, faster or more skilled than you are and have a go against him. It will place you under more pressure and will help your game. It may also help you set or reassess your goals.

Don't be frightened about trying something and making a mistake. Just make sure you learn something from that mistake. The player who is frightened about making an error won't know his limits, let alone extend them.

Evaluate your training performance as a whole but particularly in the area you identified as wanting to improve. Be honest. Most serious sportspeople keep a training diary (figure 13.1) in which they record short- and long-term training goals and their evaluation of their training. You might like to do this.

Training Diary

Week: _____   Dates: _____ to _____

Last week's game versus _____   Result Win/Loss Score: _____

Performance Rating

Component	Excellent 5	Very good 4	Pleasing 3	OK 2	Disappointing— needs work 1	Comments
Ball handling						
Gathering						
Marking						
Handballing						
Kicking						
Goal kicking						
Tackling						
Spoiling						
Team play						
Fitness						

Opponent this week: _____

Goal for this week: _____

One area I need to work on at training this week: _____

Training Session One

Date: _____

My specific goal for this training session: _____

	Very good 5	Good 4	OK 3	Poor 2	Bad 1	Comments
Overall, I am pleased with my training today						
I am pleased with my effort at training today						
I felt good at training today						
I achieved my practice goal at training today						

What I need to work on next training session or before: _____

See Steps to Success step _____

Figure 13.1 Example of a training diary.

Training Session Two

Date: _____

My specific goal for this training session: _____

	Very good 5	Good 4	OK 3	Poor 2	Bad 1	Comments
Overall, I am pleased with my training today						
I am pleased with my effort at training today						
I felt good at training today						
I achieved my practice goal at training today						

What I need to work on next training session or before: _____

See Steps to Success step _____

COACH PREPARATION FOR TRAINING

The role of the coach in relation to training sessions is pivotal. How he undertakes his preparation will be guided by a number of factors. Inevitably, he will be influenced by his own background as a player and to a lesser degree how he was coached. He will have his own goals and expectations.

A training session for juniors will not, and should not, resemble that of more senior players, let alone one for an elite team. This is the overriding principle of training. Training should be appropriate to the age, maturity, experience, skill level and realistic expectations of the playing group. Coaches of junior teams in particular have the difficult task of developing players' skills through interesting and enjoyable training drills and sessions while resisting the players' natural desire to play the game. The AFL coach, on the other hand, can make quite extraordinary demands on his professional players that would not be feasible even at the state league level. A number of principles, however, are common to all coaches in planning and conducting training sessions.

Time is the essence of training and needs to be prioritised. How are you going to use the time best and most efficiently and effectively? Are the activities you include going to contribute to the individual players' and the team's development, or have you included them because of tradition, convenience or habit? Successful coaches can't afford to waste time. Don't be hesitant to modify or even abandon altogether a training drill that is not working.

As a coach, you will need to plan ahead. The coach who thinks about his training session on the drive to the ground or as it takes place will not necessarily provide the best experience for his charges. You should have a plan of what you want to achieve and how you are going to go about it. What activities are you going to include, and in what order? How will you introduce new ones?

Your coaching plan will also involve practical issues such as the equipment you might need. How many balls will you need? Is there a need to differentiate teams and groups? How will you do this? How many markers will you need? Will

151

you need to keep score? How will this be done and by whom? What will you do with players who are unable to train?

Know the principles of teaching and learning skills. First, introduce the new skill. Demonstrate the skill and explain it briefly. Give the players an opportunity to practise the skill and provide feedback to correct errors. Finally, place the players under some pressure when using the skill to create a more gamelike atmosphere.

Don't spend too much time talking unnecessarily. Players improve by doing. Players should not be called in, given feedback and then not given another chance to practise.

Don't use training drills as punishment for poor play either at matches or during training.

Don't make threats you may not be able to keep such as, "We are going to continue doing this until we get it right!"

When players are in lines, these should not be too long. Three or four waiting their turn should be about the maximum. This will mean having sufficient balls and equipment on hand.

Make sure you evaluate training sessions. Did you and your players meet the specific objectives? This evaluation may well involve comments and suggestions from players. Keep a training diary that lists the date, plan, activities and evaluation of all training sessions. This can become an invaluable resource.

TRAINING SESSIONS

The structure of a training session will of necessity be quite different from session to session. The basic framework described here and summarised in table 13.1 will work for most situations.

Begin with a warm-up. The warm-up should be part of training. Include specific football activities such as gentle short kicks and handpassing; then go into some simple short running drills involving a football that are a little more vigorous.

Next, practise a known skill or drill. This probably is best done in two parts, first in pairs or very small groups and then using a team drill involving larger groups.

Next, introduce, teach and practise a new skill or drill. This will become the focus of the training session and will take the bulk of the time. This may involve one relatively simple activity for small groups and a more major one for the whole squad. Usually only one major activity of this type is introduced in any one training session.

Move into competitive practice. This should involve maximum activity for all players and simulated match conditions. Follow competitive practice with individual practice in which players are given some time to practise whatever they wish. Finish with a cool-down and stretch.

Table 13.1   Sample Training Session

Phase	Duration	Activities
Warm-up	10 minutes	Figure eights Bent-knee pass Shin ball Two-ball handball Lane work handball
Known skill or drill practice	10 minutes	Barrier ball One (plus one)-on-one competitive
New skill or drill introduction	20 minutes	Five point kicking with goal kicking
Competitive practice	10 minutes 10 minutes	Goal race Handball football
Individual practice	10 minutes	Players' choice
Cool-down	10 minutes	Cool-down activities Coach's review

An organised coach will have in his planning approximate timings for each of the activities as a guide. However, these should not be regarded as absolute. The coach should extend activities if players need more time to practise or curtail activities if they are too easy or too difficult for the players or if the objectives have been met.

TRAINING SUCCESS SUMMARY

Training is an integral and vital part of improving performance. More time is spent at training than in matches. In senior games, a player may touch the ball 5 to 30 times depending on the position he plays. This being the case, he cannot afford skill errors and certainly is not going to improve his skills during the game. Training is the time in which he will handle the ball many more times. During training, pressure can be reduced and a skill performance analysed and errors and techniques corrected. For a training session to be effective, it must involve planning, performance and evaluation for both player and coach. This step has been designed to help in these processes with the ultimate goal of improving performance on match day.

Conditioning

Australian football is a vigorous game that requires both a variety of skills and a high level of fitness. In senior football it is not unusual for most players to run more than 10 kilometres during a game (in fact, some do double that). At times a player will jog, but more likely he will need to sprint a distance; then he might have to sprint again before he has had a chance to recover. All of this running is done over the four quarters (two hours) of a game, requiring not only speed but also endurance. Players have to chase and be chased, which may involve twisting and turning, and they need to contest strongly in fierce contact situations by tackling and being tackled. They have to leap, be strong enough to steal the ball away from opponents, kick long distances and be able to fall and recover quickly. Therefore, all aspects of fitness and strength, speed, endurance, flexibility, power, recovery and agility are important to an Australian footballer.

Although fitness alone does not guarantee skill at the game, without sufficient fitness one cannot achieve full potential as a player. Indeed, some players compensate for deficiencies in other areas by honing their fitness.

A fit player is able to resist fatigue and perform better for a longer time. Research shows that a tired player's skill, coordination and concentration decrease. Fitness also helps reduce the frequency and severity of injury. And fit players recover from injury faster.

The fit footballer may be able to play better. Many of the game's skills require a certain level of fitness. Marking and kicking require power. The player with speed will be able to get to the ball first or avoid or apply a tackle. Strength will ensure a secure grip when tackling. Getting down to pick up the ball requires flexibility. Agility enables a player to dodge, weave and recover quickly from a fall. Skill is insignificant if a player is not fit enough to compete for and take the ball.

Although fitness is important, skill development is equally vital. If skill training sessions are well conducted, they will contribute to the players' fitness levels.

Conditioning training—particularly the heavy, concentrated work required by top-level players—is not a high priority for young players. Young football players need to develop the fitness aspects specifically related to football. One way to do this is to practise the skills of football often and under a degree of pressure; this will ensure hard work at both skills and fitness. Fitness activities should include the use of a football. For example, a running activity can include bouncing, kicking and chasing a ball. Flexibility work can include handling a football. Strength work can entail competing against a partner. Power work can involve leaping for a ball.

FITNESS COMPONENTS

Players of any sport require a basic level of fitness in the areas of strength, endurance, speed, power, flexibility and agility. The footballer builds on this basic level to develop fitness specific to football (figure 14.1).

Australian football is a game of continuous action made up of relatively short bursts of high-intensity activity followed by periods of various lengths in which to recover. This type of physical demand is placed on players for two hours; as such, it requires players to develop a certain degree of specific fitness. The game also involves heavy physical clashes and explosive, agile movements; players must prepare for these as well.

Players also need to train for their particular positions. The rover, for example, requires speed and dash along with the endurance to cover the large field. The ruckman will need strength plus an ability to move all around the field for the entire game. The half forward is at his best if he has speed, agility and spring, skills that must be countered by the half back, who also needs the strength necessary for the strong tackle, and so on. Each individual player will also have special requirements related to his level of fitness, such

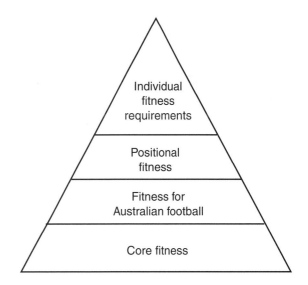

Figure 14.1 Hierarchy of fitness.

as a need to strengthen a weak shoulder or to improve flexibility for tight hamstring muscles.

A good way to determine which fitness components a particular player should work on is to make up a fitness profile like the one shown in figure 14.2. Draw such a profile for your position and rate yourself to get an idea of which fitness activities you may need to do.

	1	2	3	4	5	6	7	8	9	10
	Less important								**More important**	
Strength						*				
Speed									*	
Power								*		
Stamina									*	
Flexibility								*		
Agility								*		

Figure 14.2 Fitness component profile for a wingman.

FITNESS ACTIVITIES

Serious sportspeople will look at areas in which they need to improve and will spend time alone away from formal practice sessions working on these areas. Fitness may be an area that additional work can help. It is beyond the scope of this book to detail the principles of various fitness training methods and programs, but some simple activities are offered to give players a start towards fitness improvement.

Flexibility Exercises

Footballers need a general level of flexibility, but they need to be particularly flexible in the calves, hamstrings, quadriceps, lower back, groin and shoulders. Players should select exercises to stretch each of these areas.

When doing the stretch, do not bounce or jerk but gradually extend the muscle or muscle group until you feel the stretch. Hold that position for about 15 seconds before repeating. Footballers should stretch daily.

Calves

Push-up calf stretch: Get into the push-up position with your body straight. Place one foot on top of the other foot (figure 14.3). Now slowly rock back and try to touch the heel of your lower foot to the ground. Hold for 15 seconds. Switch feet and repeat. Do two stretches for each leg. Finish by putting both feet on the ground and walking your hands back towards your feet, keeping your legs straight, to stand up.

Figure 14.3 Push-up calf stretch.

Groin

Sitting groin stretch: Sitting with your knees bent, push the soles of your feet together and hold on to your ankles (figure 14.4). Place your elbows

Figure 14.4 Sitting groin stretch.

on the inner side of your knees and slowly apply downward pressure with your elbows. Hold for 15 seconds, relax and then repeat.

Lower Back

Knees to chest: Lie on your back, hug your knees to your chest and curl your head to touch your knees (figure 14.5). Hold for about 10 seconds and then uncurl, keeping your feet just above the ground until your legs are straight, at which point you should lower them to the ground. Repeat this five times.

Figure 14.5 Knees to chest.

Pelvic tilt: Lie on your back with your knees bent, your feet flat on the floor and your arms crossed over your chest (figure 14.6). Flatten your lower back onto the floor. Relax and repeat five times.

Figure 14.6 Pelvic tilt.

Hip–torso stretch: Sit with one leg extended and the other flexed so that it crosses over the extended leg with the foot on the ground alongside your knee. Place the hand on the same side as the bent knee on the floor, outstretched behind the body. Place the elbow on the other arm on the outside of your bent leg near the knee. Turn your upper body around towards the outstretched hand using the other elbow as a brace (figure 14.7). Hold for 10 to 15 seconds, relax and repeat for the other side.

Figure 14.7 Hip–torso stretch.

Hamstrings

Supine bent-leg stretch: Lie on your back with your knees bent and your feet flat on the floor. Put one hand behind the calf of one leg and the other on the thigh. Flex fully at the hip and gently pull on your calf until you feel a mild stretch (figure 14.8). Hold for 15 seconds, repeat and then do the other leg.

Figure 14.8 Supine bent-leg stretch.

Supine straight-leg stretch: Repeat the bent-leg stretch, but this time make sure the leg is

Figure 14.9 Supine straight-leg stretch.

straightened before flexing at the hips (figure 14.9). Keep the leg straight throughout the stretch.

Quadriceps

Kneeling quad stretch: Kneel on the floor with your knees about 10 centimetres apart and toes pointing behind you. Place both hands on your buttocks and push forwards as you gently lean back from the waist to where you feel the stretch. Hold for 15 seconds, relax and repeat.

Shoulders

Standing horizontal shoulder stretches: Stand with your feet shoulder-width apart. Hold your arms out to the sides with the thumbs pointing down. Slowly move both arms back until you feel the stretch in the front of your shoulders. Hold for 15 seconds, return to the starting position and relax. Now start with your arms out in front of your chest with the thumbs pointing up. Take your arms out and around, keeping them parallel to the ground. Feel the stretch, hold and return.

Standing vertical shoulder stretch: This time start with your arms to your sides with the thumbs pointing forwards. Take your arms straight up past your ears, leading with your thumbs. Feel the stretch, hold and return.

Strength Exercises

People immediately think of weights and gymnasiums when they think about improving strength, but the most available apparatus is your own body.

Arms and Chest

Push-ups: These can be done from the knees (figure 14.10a) or from the regular push-up position (figure 14.10b). The emphasis with both is to ensure that the body is kept straight with no sag and that it is lowered to the point that the chest lightly touches the ground. Then the body should be pushed up until the elbows are straight in the extended position. When you can do two sets of 10 bent-knee push-ups with 15 seconds rest between sets, then move up to regular push-ups building up to two sets of 10. Regular push-ups can then be made more difficult by doing them with your feet on a chair.

Figure 14.10 Push-ups: *(a)* knee position; *(b)* regular push-up position.

Abdominal Area

Abdominal curls: These are sit-ups that *must* be done with knees *bent* and feet flat on the floor without being held. Hold your arms across your chest *(do not* put your hands behind your head) and sit up until your back is about 45 degrees from the ground (figure 14.11a). Lower yourself slowly back to the ground and repeat.

Figure 14.11 Abdominal curls: *(a)* feet flat on the floor; *(b)* feet propped against a wall.

Once you are able to do 30 sit-ups relatively easily with your feet on the floor, change the exercise and place your feet against a wall so that they are straight and about 30 degrees from the floor. Extend your arms. Keep your legs straight as you sit up and try to touch your toes (figure 14.11b). When you are able to do 30 of these easily, increase the angle of the legs to the floor.

Arms

Pull-ups: Hang from a bar or a tree branch. Pull your whole body weight up so that your chin is level with your hands. Do as many as you can before quitting.

Dips: Sit with your back next to a low bench and your legs straight on the floor. Put your hands on the bench and push your weight from the floor so that your arms are straight (figure 14.12a). Lower your body back to the floor (figure 14.12b). Work towards your maximum each time.

Figure 14.12 Dips: *(a)* starting position; *(b)* lowered position.

Groin

Football squeezes: Place a football (or a pillow) between your knees and try to squash it. Don't hold your breath. After about five seconds, relax. Repeat three times.

Hamstrings

Lower the body: If you are working out with a friend, kneel on the ground with your body upright and legs straight behind you. Have your friend hold your feet and legs on the ground. (If you are by yourself, try to lock your feet under something such as a piece of furniture.) Keeping your body straight and not bending at the waist, lean forwards, controlling your rate of forward movement with your hamstrings. As you lose out to gravity, catch your body weight with your hands on the ground. Have a rest and then repeat this exercise once. Change over with your friend.

Legs

Stair climb: Climbing stairs is good for strength and helps develop endurance. If you train where there is a grandstand, run up to the back of the stand three times. Be careful coming down and just walk down the steps rather than running. If there aren't any stairs where you train, whenever you do get to a flight of stairs, run up them, or even bound up two at a time. Be careful of other users, and always walk down the stairs.

Standing jump: Do a standing jump off both feet to get as high as you can. Stand with both feet on the ground. Bend the knees so that you are able to spring high. As you leap into the air, reach up vigorously with your arms as if you were leaping for a ball. Do this 10 times with a few seconds' rest between jumps.

Bounding: Bound by either taking off and landing on the same leg repeatedly or alternating to take off from one leg and land on the other. Or try repeatedly taking off and landing on both legs. One set of each of these over 20 metres with a minute's rest between each set should be enough.

Overall Strength

Wrestling: If you have a training partner, a good overall strength exercise for contact sports is wrestling. For example, one player lies flat on the ground while the other tries (any way he likes) to prevent him from getting to his feet. The holding player gives the signal when to start. Change over.

FOOTBALL STAMINA AND SKILL TRAINING

For most players, but particularly young ones, time spent for pure fitness tasks such as running laps should be minimised. Combining skill training and fitness training is much better than separating the two.

Although AFL players have to have an extremely high level of running fitness, they also have to develop specific endurance fitness.

This is obtained through skill drills that involve a lot of high-intensity work followed by short periods of recovery, both of varying duration. The following drills are examples of skill drills that involve a lot of running but incorporate football skills. Distances set will depend on the fitness level and ages of the players. These are but a few examples of skill drills.

Skill Drill 1. *Give and Go*

Too often players handball or kick the ball and think that their job is done. This drill requires the player who has given the handball to chase after it to try to execute a tackle.

Players are in groups of five. Player A handballs to player B, who handballs to player C, who handballs to player D, who handballs to player E. All players are running forwards to the markers except for player A, who runs behind the group trying to get close enough to player E to tackle him before he reaches the marker (figure 14.13). Or, if you do not want to use the tackle, player A can run past player E to receive a handball (figure 14.13). Change positions after each run with each player having several turns at being the chaser and the chased.

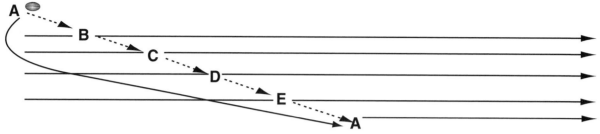

Figure 14.13 Setup for give-and-go drill.

Success Check

- Run hard to make sure you get to player E or the ball before either reaches the marker.

- All players need to run at maximum speed.
- All jog back to the starting point to repeat, but with players in different positions.

Skill Drill 2. *Three-Man Weave*

Player A handpasses to player B, who has run in front of him. Player B gives to player C. Player C gives back to player A as they crisscross until the ball is handpassed to player D, who gives to player E and so on (figure 14.14). Each player has to run wide and fast enough to ensure that the ball is always handpassed forwards. Markers can be placed to make players run wide. As players become more adept, the weave can be done with five players over a longer and wider run.

Success Check

- The ball is given and taken by players on the move and at some speed.
- The ball is handballed forwards.
- Players will have to run hard to be in position to take the ball.

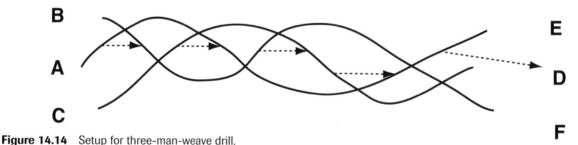

Figure 14.14 Setup for three-man-weave drill.

Skill Drill 3. *Kick-and-Run Relay*

Teams of five spread evenly around a circle or square as in figure 14.15. Player A has the ball and kicks long to player B, who marks or gathers and stands alongside the marker. Player A sprints after his kick to player B and tags player B. Player B then runs in the direction of player C and kicks to him. Player C marks or gathers and returns to wait to be tagged by player B before he runs

towards player D, kicks and follows up. The ball keeps going around the circle for a period of time set by the coach. Teams get 1 point each time they pass the starting point. The team with the most points at the expiration of time wins. The coach needs to ensure that players do not interfere with other teams' balls or leave the marker before they have been tagged.

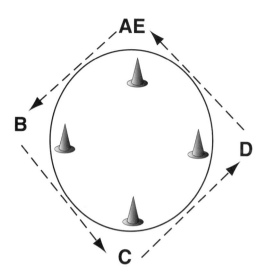

Figure 14.15 Setup for kick-and-run relay drill.

Success Check

- All kicks should be accurate.
- The player who has kicked the ball sprints hard to get to the player who has received the ball and is waiting to start running.

Skill Drill 4. *Ladder-Bounce Relay*

Players are in teams of four. Markers are set distances apart along the side of where the players will run. Teams start with two players at the start line and two level with the first marker (figure 14.16). Player A runs to player B, bouncing the ball. Player A handballs to player B, who cannot leave until tagged by player A. Player A jogs through to the second marker. Player B runs to player C, bouncing the ball. Player B handballs to player C, who waits to be tagged before running to player D. Player C handballs to player D, tags him and jogs to the second marker. Player D takes the ball down to player B. Players continue in this fashion to each of the markers in turn to the end

marker. Players can end at the end marker, or the coach may decide to have them continue down the markers with the race finishing when players get back to their starting points.

Success Check

- Players run hard between the markers.
- Once a player has handballed the ball, he keeps sprinting to tag the receiving player.
- Handball skill must be maintained.
- If the distance to be run in any one leg is greater than 15 metres, the ball will need to be bounced as in football rules.

Figure 14.16 Setup for ladder-bounce relay drill.

Skill Drill 5. *Run Rabbit Run*

Players are in teams of five. Markers are set up as shown in figure 14.17. Player A has the ball. He runs towards and handballs to player R (the 'rabbit') and goes behind player D. Player R puts the ball on the ground by the marker and runs

to the other marker. While player R is running to the second marker, player A tags player B, who runs and gathers the ball off the ground. When player R reaches the second marker, he turns and receives the handball from player B. Player R puts

DB   **R** ⟵————————⟶   **AC**

5 metres   **15 metres**   **5 metres**

Figure 14.17   Setup for run-rabbit-run drill.

the ball on the ground by the second marker and then runs back to the first marker. Player B tags player C, who runs and gathers the ball off the ground. Player R turns and receives the handball from player C. The process keeps going for a time set by the coach, who calls for the next player to become the rabbit doing the shuttle run in the middle.

Success Check

- All handballs must be accurate.
- The 'rabbit' runs hard enough to ensure that he has time to turn and receive the ball from the chasing player.
- Pursuing players will also run hard and encourage the 'rabbit'.

Skill Drill 6. *Vicious Circle*

The players stand around in a circle. They number off 1, 2, 3 and 4 until every player has a number from 1 to 4. The coach calls out a random number (1 through 4) and a direction. Players with the called number step back out of the circle and run around the circle in the specified direction. Each runner tries to catch the player running in front of him and apply a legal tackle until he gets back to his starting position in the circle. The coach continues to call numbers randomly for a set period of time so that players have numerous runs but never know when their number will be called. A variation can be 'musical balls', in which there is a limited number of balls in the middle of the circle for players to gather when they return through their starting points.

Success Check

- Running is aggressive. Try to catch the player immediately in front.
- Be alert for your number even if you are recovering from a previous run.

WARM-UP

Before every practice session or game, a warm-up will ready the body for what is to come as well as prepare the player mentally. The length of time for and intensity of the warm-up will vary according to temperature, the age and experience of the players and the type of activity to follow. At the very least, even just before a few kicks alone or with a few friends, you should stretch your legs. Then start off with short kicks before gradually making them longer. A general guide is that a warm-up should take 10 to 15 minutes. This should be sufficient time to start sweating, which is an indication that your muscles have warmed enough for action.

Generally, after a warm-up has elevated your body temperature, you should follow it with some flexibility exercises. Follow these in turn with specific football activities involving kicking, handballing, marking and other football movements. The following is an example of a suitable warm-up that could be done by you and another player or by a group of players at a match or a practice.

Activities to Elevate Body Temperature

Follow the leader: Have a ball with you and jog around the area bouncing and handballing backwards and forwards. Play follow the leader, with the front person bouncing as he runs. Change over by putting the ball on the ground or handballing in the air for the following player to take the lead. Do this for a minute or so.

Alternate foot touches: Stand with the ball on the ground between you and a partner so that you both are facing the ball with a foot on the end of the ball closest to you (figure 14.18). Now alternately touch your feet lightly on the top of the ball so that each player looks as if he is going to step down on it. But as the foot touches it, the foot is pulled quickly away and replaced by the other. Keep in time with your partner for about a minute.

Figure 14.18 Alternate foot touches.

Sideways jump–sit-up changeover: While one player does 15 bent-knee sit-ups (figure 14.19a), the other does side jumps over and back across the ball (figure 14.19b). Change over.

Figure 14.19 Sideways jump–sit-up changeover: *(a)* bent-knee sit-up; *(b)* side jump over a ball.

Roll–handball changeover: Stand alongside your partner, who rolls the ball about 5 metres away. Run smartly after it, pick it up and turn. Handball back to your partner and return to your starting position. Your partner then gives you the ball and you roll it. Have five turns each.

Flexibility Exercises

Lower leg partner stretch: Select a partner about the same size as you are. Stand facing each other with your hands on each other's shoulders. Both of you take small steps backwards, making sure that your heels touch the ground on each step (figure 14.20). When you are at a maximum distance apart, stand with both heels on the ground and hold for 15 to 20 seconds.

Figure 14.20   Lower leg partner stretch.

Figure eights: Stand with your feet a little more than shoulder-width apart, about 3 metres away from and facing your partner. Roll the ball around your body, first one way and then the other. Handball to your partner, who does the same. Repeat, but this time roll the ball in a figure-eight pattern around and between the feet (figure 14.21a). Repeat again, but keep the ball off the ground as it makes the figure eight (figure 14.21b).

Knee lifts: Pass the ball around your body at waist height (figure 14.22a). Pass it in both directions and then handball to your partner, who does the same. Repeat several times and then pass it alternately under and over your legs as you walk on the spot with a high knee lift (figure 14.22b). Don't forget to regularly handball to your partner to do the same.

a

b

Figure 14.21   Figure eights: *(a)* Roll the ball through the legs; *(b)* keep the ball off the ground as it goes through the legs.

Figure 14.22   Knee lifts: *(a)* The ball goes around body at waist height; *(b)* the ball passes under and over the legs as the knee lifts.

Twist and catch: Stand about 3 metres from and facing away from your partner. Keeping your feet still about shoulder-width apart, turn to face your partner as he also turns towards you. Handball the ball so that he can take it in his hands (figure 14.23). Both of you should revert back to the starting position. Repeat, but this time he will handball to you. Repeat, again turning in different directions.

Sitting leg stretch: Sit facing your partner with your legs extended but slightly bent and your feet pressed against the feet of your partner. Both of you hold the part of the ball closest to you as the ball rests on top of your toes. Hold for 15 seconds. Try again but with the ball turned so that you attempt to hold it at the ends (figure 14.24).

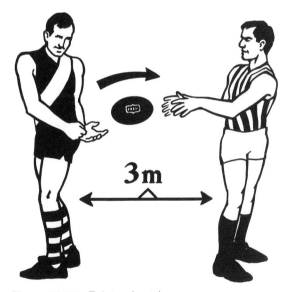

Figure 14.23   Twist and catch.

Figure 14.24   Sitting leg stretch.

Figure 14.25 Upper thigh stretch.

Upper thigh stretch: Lie on your right side and support yourself on your right forearm. Flex your left leg and hold your left ankle with your left hand (figure 14.25). Slowly pull the leg back until you feel a good stretch in the upper thigh. Try to keep your back straight. Hold for about 15 to 20 seconds and repeat with the other leg while lying on your left side.

Football Skill Activities

Low gather: Stand 2 metres from your partner and handball the ball at either of his feet. He moves towards the ball, attempts to gather it cleanly and returns the ball, trying to hit your feet. Try 10 times each.

Front-of-the-chest gather: Standing as for the low gather, each player handballs 20 times to the other, alternating the hand used and taking the ball in front of the chest.

Overhead marking: This activity is the same as the low gather, but this time lob the ball into the air so that your partner can practise overhead marking. Switch roles.

Kicking and receiving: Move back a step or two and practise kicking into the hands of your partner over a short distance. Work on guiding the ball to the foot, kicking accurately and taking the ball surely into the hands when receiving.

Kick for goal: From about 15 metres from goals or a target, one player stands the mark while the other has a kick for goal. The player who has stood the mark runs after the ball, recovers it and kick-passes it back to the kicker, who is now in a position to stand the mark. The player who recovered the ball runs past the player on the mark to receive the handball and then goes back to take his kick. Try alternate kicks in this fashion, gradually increasing the distance of the kick and the angle to the target.

COOL-DOWN

Just as a warm-up is a good idea to prepare the body and mind for practice or a game, a cool-down helps return the body to a resting state after exercise. It is important to allow your heart rate to gradually slow down while still providing sufficient blood flow to aid in recovery. Other bodily functions that are altered by activity also benefit by being turned off gradually.

A good habit is to conclude your practice with some easy jogging followed by some easy stretching of each of the major muscle groups used in the activity, including shoulders, calves, back, groin, hamstrings and quadriceps, the same areas that you stretched in the warm-up. These stretches should be done gently, without bouncing. Stretch, hold for a few seconds, then relax and repeat the stretch. The cool-down procedure will aid in recovery if the session has been strenuous and will assist in preventing muscle soreness the next day.

A good habit is to make sure that you have a drink both before and after your workout. During long sessions make sure you take drinks throughout the workout.

CONDITIONING SUCCESS SUMMARY

As we said at the start of this step, fitness is an important component of the game of Australian football. It is a fast, vigorous game involving many efforts and much body contact. Some very skilled players never make it to the elite level because they are not committed to developing and improving this side of their game. Others are able to compensate for a lower skill level by maximising their fitness capabilities. The player who pays attention to both gives himself the best chance of success and progressing with his football.

The exercises in this step should be seen as a 'top up' for fitness because if you do all skill drills often enough and under enough pressure, they will contribute to specific football fitness. Learning skills, and practising them, must take priority, particularly for younger players.

You've now reached the end of the steps in this book. Well done. But don't conclude from this that it is of no further use to you. Regardless of the level at which you play, there will be times when you might, perhaps even should, revisit parts of it to review where you are at, check on specific details and get ideas for practising or training sessions.

As we have emphasised throughout the book, the perfect player is yet to be born. It just doesn't happen. As good and awe-inspiring as Hird, Voss, Buckley, Judd, Goodes, Ricciuto, Reiwoldt, Tredrae are, the very good players at the AFL level still work very hard on their skills and their football fitness. They understand that even being in an area will give them a competitive edge over their opponents, and they work at trying to achieve that 1 percent (and more). All football skills can be improved by practice, and practice under pressure, when those skills will surely be tested. The best players talk to and use their coaches and teammates, seeking out ways to improve, to practise, and to eliminate errors and perfect team patterns. To return to the sign in our training facility—Practice is a rehearsal for performance. Players want to be better at both the individual and team elements of football. Although mental preparation is vital, you don't improve by thinking and reading. You improve by practice, practice, practice. Keep revisiting the skill practices in these steps. You will be a better player for it.

◨ Glossary

Australian football is a unique game. Like most games, it has its own language that players and spectators understand but is quite strange to those unfamiliar with it. What follows is a list of some of the more common words and expressions used in Australian football. Understanding these terms is crucial for players and helpful for spectators.

backmen—The six defenders across the full-back and half-back lines who are placed in a team's defensive half of the field.

back pocket—The position on either side of the full back on the last line of defence.

ball up—When the central umpire bounces or throws up the ball to restart the game after a scrimmage that results in a stalemate with neither team having an advantage.

baulk—A player with the ball attempting to deceive his opponent by faking a move in one direction and suddenly going in another.

behind—When the ball passes over the goal line after being touched or kicked by a defender, when it hits a goal post or when it passes over the behind line without touching the behind post. A behind scores 1 point.

behind line—The line drawn between a goal post and a behind post.

behind posts—The two smaller posts 6.4 metres outside the goal posts.

boundary line—The line that marks the boundary of the playing field. The ball must go completely over the line to be out of bounds.

boundary umpires—Two umpires who patrol the boundary line, one on each side of the field. They judge whether the ball is in play. When the ball is out of play, a boundary umpire returns it to play by throwing it in over his head towards the centre of the field.

bump—When a player uses his hip and shoulder to knock an opponent out of position. To be legitimate, a bump must not be in the back or above the shoulders of the opponent and must be made within 5 metres of the ball.

centering the ball—Directing the ball into an attacking position on the field directly in front of the goals.

central umpire—Also called the field umpire. There are two on the ground during a game. They have full control of play and award penalties in accordance with the rules of the game.

centre bounce—The umpire's bounce of the ball in the centre circle to start the game at the beginning of each quarter and to restart it after each goal.

centre circles—There are two centre circles, one 10 metres in diameter and the other 3 metres in diameter. The 3-metre circle in the centre of the ground is where the ball is bounced by the central umpire to start and restart the game. No player is to be in the centre circle until the ball has been bounced (or left the umpire's hand if he is throwing it up). The circle is divided into two semicircles by a line drawn parallel to the goal lines. The 10-metre circle is a restraining line to limit the distance of the ruckman's run-up. Both ruckmen must have both feet within this circle when the ball is bounced or thrown up.

centre square—The 50-metre square in the centre of the ground to control the number of players around the ball at a centre bounce. Only four players from each team are permitted in the centre square at a centre bounce.

charging—Colliding with an opposition player using an amount of physical force that is unreasonable or unnecessary in the circumstances, irrespective of whether the player is in possession of the football.

check side—The defensive side of a contest. Usually referred to in relation to a ruck contest.

corridor—The area arbitrarily about 50 to 60 metres wide down the centre of the oval from which there is a greater opportunity for scoring goals.

crumber—See *off hands/off the pack.*

dead pocket—A defensive area of the ground near a behind post where the ball is likely to be blown on a windy day.

downfield—Towards a team's goal.

dropping the ball—When a player is tackled and drops the ball, giving a free kick to the tackler. The spectators will call 'ball!' in anticipation of the umpire awarding the free kick.

drop punt—The kick most often used in Australian football. In flight the ball will spin backwards end over end.

fall of the ball—Where the ball is expected to come to ground following a kick. Rovers, followers and other running players will attempt to be at the fall of the ball to gather it as it comes off hands and dispose of it to their team's advantage.

50-metre circle—On many grounds a semicircle with a 50-metre radius is drawn from the centre of each goal. It is drawn to help umpires judge 50 metres for awarding a 50-metre penalty. On kickoffs from a behind, runners and trainers must stay outside the 50-metre line until the ball has been kicked off unless they are tending to an injured player.

first give—When a player takes the first option to dispose of the ball to a teammate. In senior football not doing this will often lead to the player with the ball being caught holding the ball and giving away a free kick.

flank—The part of the ground near the boundary line between the pocket and the wings.

followers—The team's ruckman, ruck rover and rover. More recently, other than the ruckman, they have been called on-ballers.

footpass—When the ball is passed to a teammate by kicking.

forwards—The six players of the full-forward and half-forward lines who are placed in a team's attacking half of the field.

free kick—The awarding of a penalty kick for an infringement of the rules. In fact, the ball does not have to be kicked but may be handpassed. If taking the kick would disadvantage the infringed team, the umpire may call 'play on!' and allow the play to continue.

front and square—The position of choice when reading the ball off hands from a marking pack. In this position, the player is balanced, is facing the pack and is in a position to go in either sideways direction to take the ball.

game plan—The strategies developed by the coach to maximise team strengths and to counter the opposition's; involves team disciplines developed during training.

gathering the ball—Taking possession of a ball that has fallen free from a marking or ruck contest or is rolling free on the ground.

goal—A goal is worth 6 points and is scored when the ball is kicked over the goal line by a player of the attacking team without the ball touching any player or a goal post.

goal line—The line drawn between the goal posts.

goal mouth—The area directly between the goal posts in front of goal.

goal posts—The two posts 6.4 metres apart between which the ball is kicked to score a goal worth 6 points.

goal square—The 6.4-by-9-metre rectangle in front of the goal posts from which the ball is kicked off after a behind is scored. The lines of the square make up the kickoff lines.

goal umpires—Umpires who judge the scoring of goals and behinds and record the scores. They signal a goal by waving two flags and a behind by waving one.

half-volley take—When the ball is gathered by the player as it hits the ground.

handball—Holding the ball in one hand and hitting it with the clenched fist of the other hand. Also called a handpass.

head of the square—The part of the goal square closest to the centre of the ground. Players on an acute angle to the goal will try to kick the ball rather than have a shot at goal.

hitting out—When players contesting a bounce, ball up or throw-in try to hit the ball to a teammate.

hitting the post—When the ball in flight hits one of the posts. If it hits a goal post, a behind is scored. If it hits a behind post, it is ruled out of bounds.

holding the ball—When tackled, if the player in possession of the ball does not dispose of it legally in a reasonable time, he is said to be holding the ball and a free kick is awarded against him. Spectators will cry 'ball!' in anticipation of the umpire awarding the free kick.

interchange players—The players of the team (in senior football, usually restricted to four) who are off the ground but available for unlimited substitution during the game. Substitutions may take place only through a designated interchange area 15 metres wide on the boundary line and are controlled by an interchange steward.

kickoff—When a player from a defending team kicks the ball back into play after a behind has been scored.

kickoff lines—The lines of the goal square.

knock on—When a player does not attempt to pick up the ball but hits it to advantage. It must not be thrown or scooped.

laws—The official playing rules established and occasionally modified by the Australian Football League.

leading—A player running to a free space and making a target for a teammate to footpass the ball is said to be leading.

loose man—A player who is not being checked by an opponent. Once teams have taken possession of the ball, they will try to create a loose man by running off their opponents.

man up—When a player is given the responsibility to cover a particular player when the opposition has gained possession of the ball.

mark—When a player catches the ball on the full from a kick. The ball must have travelled at least 10 metres and not been touched by another player.

minor score—Another name given (often by television or radio commentators) for a behind worth 1 point.

off hands/off the pack—When the ball is taken on the full as it falls free from a pack of players competing for a mark. Sometimes it is said that the ball is *crumbed;* players who specialize in this skill are called *crumbers*.

on the ball—Players who follow the ball around the ground rather than being placed in a set position are said to be *on the ball*. These are usually the ruckman, ruck rover and rover.

on the full—A free kick is awarded to the opposition whenever a team kicks the ball over the boundary line on the full—that is, without first bouncing the ball in the field of play.

oval—The playing field; usually grassed and with dimensions of 110 to 155 metres in width and 135 to 185 metres in length.

over the mark—A defensive player standing a mark or a free kick will be directed where to stand by the central umpire. If he encroaches over that mark before the ball is kicked, he will be penalised 50 metres for being over the mark.

pack—A group of players contesting the ball in the air.

palming—The action by which a ruckman tries to direct the ball from a hit-out to one of his teammates.

play on—When a player elects not to go back behind his mark after a mark or free kick but to get the ball quickly to advantage to a teammate. Anytime after the umpire calls 'play on!' the player can be tackled and if tackled will have been deemed to have had sufficient time to dispose of the ball and will be penalised for holding the ball.

pocket—The areas on the field close to the behind posts.

prior opportunity—When tackled, a player who is deemed to have had prior opportunity to dispose of the ball (such as while running and bouncing, spinning or baulking) will be penalised for holding the ball.

propping—A player stopping in front of and facing an opponent, forcing him to make his move or dispose of the ball.

push and run—If the ball is within 5 metres, a player may push off his opponent, but not in the back or face.

rocket handball—A handball in which the ball spins backwards end over end in flight. It is the preferred method for accuracy and distance.

runner—A team official who carries messages from the coach to the players during the course of the game. There are no timeouts in Australian football

running off—Usually refers to a defensive player who leaves his opponent to provide a running attacking option for his team's attack. Coaches will despair if the forward player doesn't chase his defensive opponent and fight to keep the ball in the attacking zone.

shepherding—A player using his body to block an opponent from the ball or a teammate. It is illegal to shepherd more than 5 metres from the ball.

smother—When a player uses his hands to trap the ball on an opponent's foot as he kicks.

spoil—A defensive action in which the ball is punched away from an opponent attempting to mark.

standing the mark—The player standing on the spot where his opponent has marked the ball or been given a free kick for an infringement is said to be standing the mark. He does this to ensure that his opponent does not play on and has to kick over the mark, which is a more controlled situation for the defensive team to counter.

tackle—The laws of football state that a player executes a tackle correctly if the player held is in possession of the football and is tackled below the shoulders and above the knees. A tackle may be from the front, back or side provided that a player held from the back is not pushed in the back.

tagging—Shadowing an opponent over the field with the sole object of denying him possession of the ball. Usually the player given this defensive responsibility must sacrifice his own attacking game.

taking the ball—Gathering the bouncing ball in the hands prior to a controlled disposal to a teammate.

throw-in—When the ball has gone out of bounds over the boundary line (other than after a kick on the full or directly from a kickoff), the boundary umpire will throw the ball back into play over his head towards the centre of the ground.

torpedo punt—A kick that causes the ball to spiral through the air; sometimes called a screw or spiral punt.

tumble pass—A handball in which the ball tumbles forwards end over end in flight. If it goes to ground, it will bounce away from the player.

turnover—Losing possession of the ball to the opposite team.

◨ About the Authors

Andrew McLeod has played in the Australian Football League (AFL) for a decade and is one of the most popular and talented players in the game. A life member of the Adelaide Football Club, McLeod has exceptional skills and blinding speed that have made him a fan favourite to legions of Crows supporters as well as opponents and football followers.

McLeod has received numerous accolades, awards and medals. He is a three-time All-Australian as well as a dual winner of the Norm Smith medal, which is awarded to the AFL Grand Final's most outstanding player. In 2004, at the age of 28, McLeod reached another significant milestone when he played his 200th senior game. McLeod has been named club champion twice, runner-up three times and third once. He has regularly placed as a top-10 contender for the AFL's Brownlow Medal, including a second and third placing. McLeod also won the Michael Tuck Medal for the most outstanding player in the preseason championship game in 2003.

Trevor Jaques has gone from representing South Australia as a schoolboy and amateur footballer to serving as fitness coach for the SA team, which won the 1988 and 1993 Australian championships. He has played, taught and coached at many levels and served as an elite-level fitness coach for more than 25 years. With this extensive background, he has at various times held positions as fitness director, runner and team selector for the Adelaide Football Club, in the Australian Football League, since the team's inception in 1991. For the past 12 years he has served as the league's training services manager, the position he currently holds.

Jaques received his bachelor's degree and physical education qualifications from Adelaide University and his master's degree from Michigan State University. Formerly a senior lecturer in sport sciences at the University of South Australia, Jaques taught sport and skill analysis, sport injuries, sports conditioning and football.